DON'T
CHANGE THE CHANNEL

The Wisdom And Story Of A Spiritual Channel

And

The Teachings Of His Guide

BY:

BLAIR STYRA

WITH

TABAASH

OZARK
MOUNTAIN
PUBLISHING

For permission, serialization, condensation, adaptions, or for our catalog of other publications, write to Ozark Mountain Publishing, Inc., P.O. box 754, Huntsville, AR 72740, ATTN: Permissions Department.

Library of Congress Cataloging-in-Publication Data

Styra, Blair – 1960

Don't Change the Channel by Blair Styra

This book is about life on all levels of Mind, Body, & Spirit. Blair shares his journey as he develops his ability as a channel for Tabaash.

1. Channeling 2. Tabaash 3. Spirit Guidance 4. Metaphysics

1. Styra, Blair, 1960 II. Tabaash III. Title

Library of Congress Catalog Card Number: 2014941219

ISBN: 9781940265063

Cover Design: enki3d.com

Book set in: Times New Roman, Bradley Hand

Book Design: Tab Pillar

Published by:

PO Box 754

Huntsville, AR 72740

800-935-0045 or 479-738-2348 fax: 479-738-2448

WWW.OZARKMT.COM

Printed in the United States of America

DEDICATION

I would like to dedicate this book to Kay whose life journey has been the template for so much of who I am…

And to my dear friends Marion and Martyn Rix whose love and support has been a great gift to me.

Table of Contents

TENA KOE!
Greetings!

In the 1980s when I was in my twenties, I once again picked up the thread of my spiritual self, gave it a good shake, and reconnected it to my human nature. That thread was always there, of course, but like so many threads of life, we can only make that link again once we have lived up to a certain point in the experiences of the life that we are living. From that point, we begin to "create" new ways of being on all levels. One thing that really struck me and made so much sense in my creating was the idea that we are all GOD. For me, it was not a revelation but a knowing that made so much sense to my whole being in all ways.

Some years later I was interviewed on National Radio here in New Zealand, and the interviewer asked me what my philosophy was, and so, on National Radio, I announced to the whole country that I believed that we were all God and that we were all here to help each other remember this and live in this way. The announcer was rather shocked and for quite a few seconds said nothing. I carried on talking and then at some point she said that what I said made sense.

Such an announcement on that level made a huge impact on my life as a channel as it opened up yet another mass of doors of my own development and the direction my work would take me. I had "created" yet another new reality.

This book is about some of my human life and the God that I am and how I came to be a channel for an extraordinary, personable spiritual entity known as Tabaash. We write this as Gods together beginning with a brief introduction by each of us—this one is mine and Tabaash's follows. Then we each write a chapter, the first one is from me, and the second chapter is contains Tabaash's words.

TABAASH SPEAKS

I am Tabaash Salaam Mayhem and like you I once lived in a body. Now I am known in human terms as a "disembodied entity." Like you though, I am simply consciousness consisting of all that is life, all that you know as GOD. Participating in this journey with Blair is my choice. It is a choice that I am exceedingly pleased to be a part of as it offers many opportunities to show to human nature "the God nature," which, of course, is your true nature. Through the many lives that I had lived, I inevitably lived up to a place where I understood the true environment of the soul, and so I endeavoured to live my life in such an environment. And being not just physical, this setting offered an immense potential that otherwise would never have been experienced.

Living life at this time is not a hard task; it is an honest one born of the choice you made to be alive at a time of such exaggerated and amplified experience. Your life and all that it portrays to you are the deals that you have made and continue to make every moment of your existence in both physical and non-physical realms. The God Nature is manifest more than ever at this time in your history NOT because you need to be saved and taught better ways but because as a collective Being of Energy, you have all simply evolved to the place where you are now able to BE GOD on a conscious level. My own self-energy and any who work in this way to assist are simply directing you back to your Authentic Self.

Only you can be your own Authentic Self. Decide what makes YOUR soul sing and find the ways to live this.

Tabaash

CHAPTER ONE

BLAIR'S STORY

I am the poet of the body. I am the poet of the soul.

Walt Whitman

Of course, it would be totally appropriate if I could start this story by telling you that I was born in a halo of golden light, spirit incarnate consciously, bringing great reverence and joy to all who beheld me at my birth. Since, of course, this is completely untrue, it would be deemed highly inappropriate to do so and would no doubt initiate many questions and comments from people who were more highly informed about the circumstances of my birth so it is best to stick to the facts.

Styra boy, born October 12, 1960, 8:55 AM; Royal British Columbian Hospital; New Westminster, Canada; 8 pounds 5oz. The doctor who delivered me went by the interesting name of Dr. Pepper that I think is totally fitting! Apparently I was born with my feet turned up which I suppose one could make many an assumption about. As it is, I have always had ankles that rather click when stretching. My father was of Ukrainian descent, and my Mother was Swedish, Welsh and Spanish. I was the second of four children and the eldest of three sons. So having made once again the deal to return to Earth, I began my journey of this lifetime.

My first five years were a fairly predictable blend of the life of a child being that was fairly defined and interpreted by the lives of the people who were closest to me. I do recall quite specifically my first day of school: feeling apprehensive but also liberated as the world opened another door for me. My lunch pail was a square box with a handle, and it had a tartan design on it. For whatever reason—only known to the mind of a five year old boy—I thought it would make an exceedingly good missile and recall throwing it over a very steep bank much to the consternation of my poor mother who had the arduous task of climbing down the bank and retrieving it for me!

We also had to bring with us a rug that we would lie upon "to rest" as it said on the list. My young mind at the time conjured up images of intense learning followed by rigorous playtime sessions which ended up with us all mentally and physically exhausted, collapsing onto our prescribed rugs "to rest." Mine was a brick red with black flecks, and it had a red fringe and a rubber back. I pretended that it was a magic carpet that would fly me anywhere I wanted to go.

From the time I was exposed to school, away from the protective armour of my parents' lives, I became aware that my peers seemed to be uncomfortable around me and, therefore, isolated me. In response I created a wall around me to protect myself, and by doing so, I attracted verbal and at times physical abuse. I liked talking to adults, but most of them didn't know what to make of this five year old who preferred the company of adults instead of his own peers. So sensing their hesitation in regards to me, I felt more isolated. I walked around the school at recess and lunchtime with a teacher who was the monitor, which, of course, hardly helped me make friends and influence my own age group!

Through those early grade school years I would without question allow my young mind to be guided and directed by the teachers who changed as the years went by. Some were quite excellent and sensitive as teachers, others not so.

My fourth grade teacher, for instance, had to give me extra math tutoring after school on some days, and she in all probability detested those sessions as much as I positively loathed them! I'm sure she was a very good person, but she had a short fuse, and if I deemed to get anything wrong, she would wack me and call me "a very stupid boy." This was never a relationship made in heaven, and her methods of teaching me were hardly going to prime me for a Pulitzer Prize in mathematics! The more she verbally abused me and wacked me, the more defiant, upset and tearful I became. And so we battled on, she and I, week after week until the sessions abruptly ended. I never knew why; I simply accepted they did with great relief and never looked back. Maybe she became fed up with me and refused to do anymore or perhaps the overtime wasn't all it was cracked up to be. Whatever the case, I was free!

Another thing about her that stands in my mind is that she, like many women in the 1960s, wore a girdle, and the boys of the class would be constantly dropping their pencils when she walked by up and down the aisles in the classroom. She would always pick them up and when she did, she would never bend her knees; she would simply bend at the waist consequently giving us an eyeful!

As young people, we so readily accepted the adults and the world that they lived in, and we trusted them to interpret this world and all it had to offer. I never thought of teachers as people with lives of their own with children and husbands or wives. I just saw them as teachers who were there when I arrived and because of this, I simply assumed that they must have lived at school. It never entered my mind that they would pop home at the end of the day kick off those stilettos and get that girdle off. They were simply always there when I went to school.

This idea was totally shattered when this same fourth grade teacher was leaving to have a baby. I was stunned! My reality had been shattered, and I had to rearrange my mind in regards to her and other teachers. Having excised the old beliefs, I had to negotiate with myself a new deal. As children, we do that constantly through instinct and I believe self-preservation. As we evolve through our early experiences, we become more aware of how we need to constantly change the strategies of life.

Children are excellent strategists as they come from a true authentic place—natural in their awareness of creating life without reason, without purpose. There is simply a need to explore, create and live. So off went this teacher who subsequently ended up having twins—served her right for being mean to me!

I never believed that there was anything particularly significant about me, but I began to sense that the way I felt and saw the world was rather different from the way other people of my age. When I look back now at the first eleven years of my life in Canada, I would sum myself up by saying that I was anxious and fearful, defiant sensitive and creative, and for my age sophisticated. I could get angry and prone to the odd fit of temper. I had the sentiment that there was a great deal more to life than I could define

When we moved to New Zealand in the 1970s, I became a server in our local church. One day I said to the priest that I thought there was more to God than what the church depicted. He asked me what I meant so I told him I thought that the priest and ministers and church leaders didn't know themselves what it was all about and that God was more than they understood. By the look on his face, I noted that he was not about to engage in a theological decision with a child who had obviously grown four heads for asking such a question and speaking in the way I did. So obviously I wasn't going to get any answers from him. You see, I knew that God really existed, but I also knew that the way God existed was different from what we were being taught by the church, and I felt that there was something in me that sensed the answer but was not quite ready to know it at that time in my life.

In Canada we lived in Port Coquitlam, a part of greater Vancouver. To get where we lived, you had to drive up a long straight road that eventually took you up the "Big Hill." Then you would keep driving a couple of minutes and then turn first on your right and then the first left after that and drive a bit more and the second house on the left was ours: 3951 Woodway

Street. If you didn't make the initial right hand turn and continued driving up the road, you would go further up into the mountains. There was a wood of pine trees on the left and houses on the right. The road turned sharply at the top where you would get into denser mountain area. On the left of that sharp turn was "the cliff," whereas kids we used to sit on the edge with our legs dangling over as we threw stones and made up stories of gruesome deaths, involving people who had fallen over the edge and been smashed on the rocks below! The view before us was spectacular, offering us a wide river with boulder-lined shores and massive forests of pines, a wild and fairly untamed landscape.

Years and years later I Google-earthed the same area and was dismayed to find in its place massive sub-divisions, the river gone. We used to walk along that river in the summertime and search for arrowheads and float down the river on inner tubes, the water a dark mossy green and so cold it would shoot your 11 year old testicles into hibernation for hours, well at least until you were warm again.

Across the road from "the cliff" was "the cemetery." I was fascinated by this place and spent a great deal of time there from as early as I can recall. I would go up there often, walk around the graves by myself, and feel a peace and energy that was not outside the cemetery walls. I had no idea how to define what I was feeling at that point, but it was somehow attached to the feeling I had that there was something "more."

There the grass was always more lush and green. It was so full of serenity and order, something that I have always appreciated. An air of great contentment was evident which I revelled in as if my soul was recognizing a way to feed a yearning for something that I could not explain but knew was not connected to my human nature.

At the far left hand side of the graves there was a little hill with very green grass and four large pine trees. There was something about those trees and that small grassy hill that brought out in me a deep sense of longing for a place that I knew. It was a feeling that went far beyond any human nature experience I'd had so far; it made me sad and joyful at the same time. I would sit up there and sometimes weep for something that seemed to be lost to me—and yet it felt like I still had it. When I sat up there, I would feel like I was looking into another place, and I could see in my mind wide expanses of country with sky so blue and sun always golden and warm. It brought out in me longing that made my soul ache for something forgotten. It was not something to be shared—that experience—as it seemed only mine, and I knew that others would not see what I was seeing and would not understand what experience I was having.

I have thought about this so often in my adult life, and as I began to understand more of my God nature, I knew that it was either me remembering the spirit world or having some kind of past life recall. And even now as an adult, occasionally in the weirdest of places I will find my grass hill with the trees, and I will be transported back to that place. Once on a roadside on a busy street in England, surrounded by the noise of loud and invasive the traffic, I have found such a place as I was walking to the gym. I stood at this place, and the sounds of the traffic vanished—I was there.

We all have these places, I believe; it's our soul recalling God and the places that connect us with that energy. I believe we all visit them frequently on both conscious and subconscious levels, particularly when we are in distress and have conflict in our lives. We search for these places, knowing that somehow they will carry us through what we are going through and knowing that in some way they will make better the messes that we find ourselves at times involved in.

In the cemetery there was one particular grave that I was always drawn to. It was the grave of the Reverend Harrison's daughter. As a child you to tend to relate death as something that happens to adults, mostly the elderly or the sick. I knew theoretically that people of all ages died, but here was actual evidence that this happened to a young person. And "I" was young and to my young mind, it all seemed so "tragic," and we were all in danger of death. And life was such a precarious thing, and it was all distressing and sad! What was it about the fact that she had died that so touched me? I never knew her, of course, but had only heard about the Reverend Harrison's dead daughter, and that seemed to awaken something up in me.

"She's buried in the cemetery." I would stand by her grave and whisper "The Reverend Harrison's dead daughter, she died and she was young."

I was fascinated by the fact that she was dead, and I knew that being dead meant something more than your body buried in a cemetery. The spirit of this young girl must have been either highly amused or somewhat perplexed at this young boy paying so much homage to her mortality!

Looking back now, I know that I was simply attuned to the spirit energy of the place. The child in me knew that it had nothing to do with human nature, and I wasn't in the least bit afraid. While I was there, I also realized that I wasn't a person. I was more; even now writing that brings tears to my eyes. When there was a funeral cortege driving up that long road to the cemetery, I would hide in the bushes in the hope of seeing "the hearse" and hopefully see "the coffin" because inside the coffin was "the body," and it was "dead."

In the 1960s, the hearses of the day were sinister-looking black Cadillac's with velvet ruche curtains at the windows—all great fodder for my undeniable Gothic mind.

I was also fascinated with people's grief and the way the energy of life seemed suspended as people lived out their losses. The raw almost primordial energy of people's grief intrigued and attracted me in some odd way. I felt like they were exposing some true aspect of themselves, an aspect that was habitually put to rest as the routines of day-to-day life took them away from something that was more real than what they normally exposed.

Interesting to note that my earliest childhood memory is of being at a funeral. I must have been two or three, and I was sitting on the grass under a big table that was laden with flowers. It was a warm sunny day, and there was not a cloud in the sky as I recall, looking up and squinting in the sun. I had on a little suit of black shorts and a black waistcoat over a short-sleeved white shirt. From where I sat, I saw lots of pairs of men and women's legs. High-heeled shoes, men with pressed trousers and polished shoes—all the people gathered round in a circle. There were a lot of people, and everything was all hushed, and I could hear birds in the trees.

It felt so serene and at peace even though I knew people were sad. I have no idea at all whose funeral it was, though as I write this the thought of my Swedish Great grandfather comes to mind.

The first 5-7 years of our lives seem interpreted by the thoughts, experiences and attitudes of others. More often this interpretation is too often clouded by the conditioning of the people whom we grow up with, and, of course, this is not always beneficial to us. I believe children have a very honest and unguarded way of approaching, seeing and experiencing the world, as they are still very attuned to the God nature.

To this day I still find solace in a cemetery though I don't make a habit of frequenting them!

TABAASH SPEAKS

You are all Gods and you come from God, and when you make the choice to once again be incarnate, the messages that you will bring will be the way that you live and the way that you will think and feel and participate. It is the same for all that exists—be it in human form, animal, mineral, plant, the gases, in fact, all that is carries the vibration of God and, therefore, all is living.

The soul is not a "human soul;" it is a force of energy that exists in all places at all times, and this energy force has the free will to take on any form of life that it chooses. When it does so, it desires that experience so it may be fulfilled in that way. How you come to be who you are now was a choice that you made and are constantly making as you live the life that you do. There is an old saying that says, "Wherever you go, you will find yourself." If you think of the implications of such a statement in regard to your possible futures, it would seem rather imperative that you would pay a great deal of consideration to your thoughts words and deeds! You make choices about your life and lives not just when you are out in spirit but while you still live, as it is the actions and thoughts and patterns you create through your living on all levels that determines the possible futures that you will experience. This life you live now is a vibration of everything, and this energy is pulsing out of you all the time, establishing yourself more in the grander scheme of collective energy. As you continue to expand the idea of what you understand as real, then you access more of the power of God and consequently become more of the creator on a conscious level. Let us speak thoughts to you on the process of "choosing" another life on Earth.

For the majority of souls who are incarnate on Earth, it is because they have had other incarnations on this planet, thereby establishing an emotional link with the energy of Earth and other souls who are doing the same thing. Some people are of the belief that being on Earth is some sort of punishment for past life sins or a place where you have to atone or learn your lessons before you can move onto the next level of consciousness. This is a completely misleading notion, and it has never been like this.

You are always God and will always be so. As you become attached to your human experiences, you move away from your authentic self, therefore, denying yourself of the boundless power of God. This stops you from being a true creator, but all have the choice through their evolution to once again live as an authentic being of energy without any boundaries.

Imagine now that you are in spirit, and you feel that once again it is time to reincarnate on Earth. The moment you experience the feeling to do so, certain souls will present themselves to you. These souls will assist you in making the choices that best serve you in the life you are creating.

These souls will guide you through a deep meditative process that will enable you to access information about yourself. This process enables you to observe past and future. From the past you choose material that is relevant to things that you feel are incomplete or certain things that may have been left unresolved, but you may also choose from the past, times when you were happy and successful and may wish once again to connect with certain souls or certain places that hold great significance to you. You are shown all your futures of that new life, and all they will indicate and from there you choose the futures that are most pertinent to what you wish to accomplish in that life.

In this place you will also choose who will parent you and if you will have siblings or not. You will map everything out right to the finest detail, but regardless of this, it is not irrevocable since there are many futures, and as you live life, you may often change direction.

Whatever direction you take though, you would still have set all of this up in spirit before you were born. A soul knows everything as a force of energy, and it is this that it is conscious of when it makes its plans. The parents and people are forces of energy. Places, schools, and events—absolutely all of life is an energy, and the soul will align itself in its plans with energy that it knows will evolve it. There is no right way. There is no wrong way. There is only the way of that soul and the wisdom in the choices that it makes. Those souls that assist will guide the soul into making the choices that will best serve that lifetime. They are there to assist in making the best deal.

Having set up the deal, you then move into another meditative state where you begin your link with the parents that you have chosen. Through this whole process, you are constantly monitoring everything. At any time you may change your mind and go back to the drawing board, so to speak. If a soul has conceived, it can access in and out of the physical body whilst the mother is still pregnant. During this "time," the soul is watching the events of life on Earth and the events of the parents on all levels as this soul will be born into all these environments, and it wants to ensure that it all fits in with its plans.

If a soul for whatever reasons decides that the plan is not going to work, and it has already conceived, then this is where a miscarriage occurs. Or the agreement that was made with the souls of the parents may permit a termination, and if this occurs, there is never ever any life force in the body because the soul would have departed. A stillborn child is no different—the soul has gone, but the karma all round established the experience. Also, a baby having been born may hover between the worlds as the soul is still monitoring its choices. To some this may sound unfeeling and rather clinical, but a soul is not caught up in emotional choices. A soul deals with the facts of the choices it makes and wants the best deal!

You do have emotional contracts with the people that are your family and friends; that's why they are who they are. You all have a collective contract with each other to serve each other and to remind each other in some way that you are all Gods together on Earth, adventuring, exploring, loving and creating. It is this energy that pulls you all together; it is getting too caught up in your human nature that separates you all.

Now having settled into your new body and having at last been born, you begin the adventure of the expression of that new life.

From the time you conceive, you have pushed *go*, and the journey begins to unfold. You are all born as your authentic self, despite what physical or mental reality you may experience. Physical and mentally disabled people are still their authentic selves, and the journey they have chosen is all part of the deal that they have made. As I said before, your message to the world is simply the life that you will lead and when you finish that message, you will return to the energy of spirit. I believe only in life some live in a physical reality and others as energy—whatever the choice—you are as soul always God.

CHAPTER TWO

We are who we are because of who we have been. It is never our destiny but always our choice.

Tabaash

From the bottom of the big hill ran a dense pine forest that continued up the left hand side. This forest went far up past the cliff and the cemetery and farther up into denser forest. As children, we were absolutely prohibited to venture into the forest or the "big bush" as we called it. Of course, the fact that we were forbidden meant that we spent a great deal of time in there, having adventures, exploring and riding our bikes through the open spaces in the forest. I loved the constant coolness and freshness and the silence that was punctuated by birds and the sound of the wind blowing through the upper canopy of the trees. The earth itself put out a pungent spiciness, mingled with other wonderful scents and aromas of nature. Cool green dark shadows and hushed places created a magical feeling of something that was forever and would never stop. When it was sunny, the sun would filter through the trees, casting light beams on the ground, giving the impression that the trees were surrounded by halos of light. It was all bathed in a deep silence that spoke to me of something more powerful and alive that was a greater part of me even though at the time I could only feel the idea of that and not articulate it into words. I would walk through this forest often and unaccompanied, allowing my thoughts to go beyond what my life was at the time.

I suppose I was meditating really but was unaware at the time there was such a thing. We are, all of us, often drawn into places that stimulate in us an ability to go deeply within ourselves and, therefore, listen to something higher. As souls, we are everything and everywhere, and that authentic self is forever and a day, looking for more ways of inviting in more of what it knows to be. It knows that there is always more of everything that is good and grand and wonderful, and it really wants a great feast of all this knowing. As a child wandering through the forest, I really felt that I was so much more and in that place everything that my life was seemed to make complete sense. It was as if I was looking at everything and understood in one feeling.

In that place I was never diluted by any form of human nature. I was my complete and total authentic self as soul. The forest gave to me a feeling that this was the way it all was with its fresh energy and life. It embraced me as if I was it and gave up to me itself completely and with an acceptance that felt natural. It was the formula of life, and I was that formula, and whilst I was there, I was simply playing the part that I had created for myself to play a very long time ago, and in this place I knew the script off/by heart.

It was belonging without longing.

And, of course, there was the mad woman, or so I was made to believe by friends with over active imaginations. I was never sure if there was just one or that the forest was amass with them. On many occasions when I was walking through the forest, I did make a concerted effort to find evidence of one. I mean, why were they mad and why were they being mad in the forest? Was it actually being in the forest that took them to this insanity? Now if I had actually come upon one or two of these "supposed mad women," I'm not unerringly sure what I would have done.

Would I have asked them the reasons for their insanity? How did they survive in that forest, and did they go to the shops? Where were their families—you know, the usual questions that children would ask should they come across a mad woman or two in a forest.

If someone said to me, "Don't go in there, or don't do that," it rather made me compelled to want to do the opposite, and it was so with these mad women. They were rather like the red rag to the bull for me. I never thought for a moment that I would ever come to any harm, and I never had an image of them dripping saliva over cracked lips and ragged faces leering at me, tearing at their hair with great pendulous breasts swaying. I always imagined them in some sort of white filmy nightgown, long flowing hair, looking sad and sighing and moaning a great deal. They, of course, always had bare feet. Actually I think they were rather like Raquel Welch in the film *One Million Years BC*. Imagine, a forest full of mad Raquel Welches, wandering through the forests of mountain suburbia, damp clinging sheer garments, flowing hair and claw like talons painted blood red, of course. There used to be a TV show on in the 60s called *Dark Shadows* all about a vampire and his bevy of nightgown clad female vampires so it's more than likely that I picked up my imagery from that!

At times friends would be with me in the forest, and when they were, the forest never spoke to me in the same way it did when it was just me there. It seemed then more silent and shut off, withdrawing something from me and seemingly without the same degree of life. So we played our childhood games making plans and feeling the freedom and the lack of responsibility that was so a part of our young lives. And when we heard our mother calling our names we would all run.

The mothers would simply stand at the back or front door and call out the names of their children. It was a chorus that had to be heeded, and you could hear the growing agitation in some of the mothers' voices if you didn't heed the call!

My own mother carried on this tradition even when we moved to New Zealand. The little two year old Alexander who lived next door to us in Auckland would call out our names after my mother did, and it really was funny having this child's voice ringing out through the neighbourhood calling our names!

Oh yes, before I forget, there was the Dumphies' house. It stood alone and had done so for many years surrounded by land that was subdivided and up for development, but for the moment, all this empty land simply exposed the Dumphies' house and, of course, as children, we just knew it must be haunted.

I have completely no idea who the Dumphies were and even why the house was empty and had been left in such a state for all those years. As long as we lived in the area, it was always like that, and when we left to move to New Zealand, it was still empty even though houses had been built on the surrounding land. It wasn't even an old house at the time; it was two stories and had very dirty windows. My mates and me used to dare each other to have a look in the windows in case one of us might "SEE" something, and if you didn't have a look, you would be a chicken or worse—a girl. I would walk by the house often on my solitary wanderings through the neighbourhood—staring hard from a safe distance daring the house to disclose its morbid secrets to me, wanting it to prove its *hauntedness* to me in some way. One day I actually took the plunge and peered into the basement windows expecting to be and scarred for life having witnessed the awful and terrible scenes that my young eyes had beheld. And so I was bitterly disappointed to see empty dusty rooms and the nothingness that was there—instead of mutilated corpses hanging by the rafters oozing blood and entrails. Well, after that, it just became another house. What a letdown!

I did sense though that it was a lonely place and that it had not been a happy home for the people who had lived there. It was a home filled with the energy of the past unhappy events still remained in the very fibre of the building. Even today I'm always aware of the energy of a house, a building, and a place. We leave the imprint of our emotions wherever we go, and we also absorb the energy of everything and everyone around us— some more than others. Our souls though have an energy mechanism that filters out most of what we absorb, but there are times when we feel it essential to our well-being to somehow purge ourselves of unwanted energy. I find that as we evolve into our more authentic selves, it becomes easier to be clear of unwanted vibrations; however, it's still a good idea to daily do a little bit of clearing. Every night before I sleep, I empty myself of the energy of the day. I will now share this with you.

From the Lord God of my being, I empty myself—mind, body, spirit—of all the energy and events of this day, and I return it back to you God with gratitude and love.

Nice and simple, and I feel it really cleans the slate of the day. As a channel that is seeing so many people through the week, I find this essential, as by the end of the day I really have absorbed the energy of people and the issues they bring with them. There are times when such a heavy energy is left behind that it can give me quite a headache and also make me feel off centre until I clear myself. Some clients come with such unconscious emotional demands at times, and I can feel my soul being sucked and pulled and poked and prodded! All of us absorb so much from our day to day living, and we really are not created to have to carry such an emotional weight, so we have to find ways of ensuring that we don't allow ourselves to do so; otherwise, we get a build-up of energy that can throw us off course and unsettle our lives. I deem it a necessity that we all do our nightly clearing, bit like flossing the soul after brushing!

Sensing the energy of people, places and events was something I was aware of as I was growing up; gradually, sometimes it developed into knowing what was going to happen. Like lots of lads my age I was a Cub Scout, and it was nearing the time when new pack leaders were going to be chosen. One day at school I had the thought and then the overwhelming feeling that I was going to be made a pack leader. In fact, I was certain it was going to happen. It was this complete knowing that overtook any idea; it was fact! I said nothing to my parents, and my parents had said nothing to me about it, but that night at the meeting I went right up to the head honcho and asked outright if I was going to be made a pack leader. She looked at me in surprise and then laughed saying, "You must have pipes for ears!" Apparently at the same time that I had the "feeling," she had been on to the phone to my mother, telling her that I was to be made a leader.

I could also tell how people were feeling by the way I sensed the energy in them. At times I would answer a question someone was going to ask me before they actually asked me. It freaked out some people and did not endear me to my peers! More isolation!

I recall an incident when we were at a Woodward's Department Store in Vancouver. The folks were perusing the goods, and as kids we were amusing ourselves as best we could. The door of an elevator opened and out came a lady who walked with the aid of crutches as she had only one leg. She was very well-groomed and had one beautiful leg with a nylon and high heeled shoe. When I looked at her, the image came into my mind of a car accident where she had lost the other leg—and then, of course, I HAD to wonder what she did with the other side of the nylon— was it casually dangling under her dress? I did look behind her to see if I could see any tell-tale signs but saw nothing. And shoes—could she go to a shop and actually buy just one shoe? The possibilities that were opening up here were enormous.

I must mention at this point my very brief career as the neighbourhood arsonist though this was not an intentional act but one created out of panic! It had been a very hot dry summer, and the heat of the constant sun bleached the grass and trees. Next door to our house was an acre of land that was bush and trees. It was no doubt going to be developed, and I had no idea at the time that I was about to speed up this process! One afternoon with nothing better to do and perhaps with unconscious mischief on my mind, I raided one of the kitchen drawers and found some rather exciting looking matches.

My mother came into the room and said in that suspicious mother voice, "What are you doing in there"?

I gave her the standard child's reply when you are definitely up to some sort of mischief, "Nothing."

I quickly pocketed the matches without her seeing before she shooed me out of the house and outdoors.

So with my booty in my pocket, I went into the bush next door to give this treasure some serious examination. The stems of the matches were covered in a thin film of wax, and the match head was a bulbous green. I had never seen matches like this before, and so, of course, I just "HAD" to light one.

It flared up and took absolutely ages to burn much to my satisfaction. I lit a few more and then after a while was satisfied. The novelty had worn off by then, and I was bored. Well, maybe just one more, and at the same time some great compulsion arose inside of me that wondered how quickly a bit of grass would burn since it was so dry.

I lit a small clump of grass and watched as the flames took flight. Of course, within moments most of the grass around the area I had lit, having been starved of any sort of moisture for months, suddenly came to light in a dance of flames.

Me? I was doing another sort of dance as I jumped up and down in desperation, trying to extinguish what I had started. It was a futile exercise, and so I did what any sensible child would do in such circumstances. I fled!

"Mum, I'm just going over to my friend, Gordy's"!

I ran as fast as I could to my friend's place not DARING to look back should I be faced with a solid wall of flames. Sodom and Gomorrah, it was not, but I was not taking any chances, pillars of salt and parental punishments ran through my mind. After about five minutes at my friend's place I heard the unmistakable sound of a fire engine rather close by.

"I wonder what's going on?" my friend ventured to ask.

I gave a rather non-committal grunt and tried to draw his attention away from topics of an unpleasant nature. It was no use. As we heard yet another siren, I had visions of incarceration in homes for seriously deranged and dangerous boy arsonists, beatings and living on cabbage soup—not to mention the years of shame and guilt that I would have to live down and that would no doubt haunt my young mind for the rest of eternity! Youthful curiosity on the other hand got the better of my fear, and so I left my friend's place and in trepidation and astounded at my own daring, I went back to the scene of the crime. On arrival I could see that the whole bush had been reduced to cinder and that the firemen were still damping down the hotspots. My mother was out there doing her bit with the garden hose.

In all curiosity and innocence, I went up to one of the firemen and asked what had happened. He explained that in these long dry summers the heat can ignite all this dry grass and wood, and he said they had put out quite a few spontaneous fires like this.

"Really?" I replied all in wonder with my most cherubic of smiles.

"Yes," he replied. "You wouldn't want to be lighting matches around this stuff."

I thought it rather wise to depart at that stage.

TABAASH SPEAKS

And so once again you find yourself experiencing life in a body of your choice in a life of your choice with all that goes with what you have created. It is neither good nor bad; it is exactly the way that you have planned it. All human beings are born with the God nature and that nature never ever leaves them through the whole life they live. From the moment you draw your very first breath, you begin your conscious experiences on Earth—the deals that you set up begin to unfold, and you start to recognize the possibilities that could be your futures.

Imagine for a moment that you are standing still and attached to you are millions and millions of thin threads of light. They emerge from every part of you, and then imagine that all these strands of light are attached to people, places, and thoughts and feelings. All these strands of light are, in fact, attached to everything that exists—not just on this Earth but all that exists. What you are experiencing is your attachment to all of life and source energy that makes life active. And this is the same for all of everything. There is nothing that you are detached from; there is nothing that you are not.

So consider this for the moment. You are a soul in your human body and how you look and feel and think, how your personality is. All that you are is a choice that you have made. Your life has been and will always be an accumulation of deals that you made so that you are able to evolve as the God that you are. Each soul carries a particular vibration that is relevant to your growth. That is why one seemingly attracts certain things, etc., that others do not. The vibration that you are is defining itself daily and defining your relationship with the world and all that you are creating it to be for yourself. Your unique vibration is your own personal magic that you use to create life. You possess all the power of God; therefore, you are no different than God. The positioning of yourself in life and the positioning of life before you is no random act. There is never any decision that is made by outside influences; there is nothing that is in control of you. You live your life guided by your conscious self and your subconscious self. You access information both from physical aspects of yourself and non-physical aspects of yourself. The people that you bring into your life and the roles they play in your life are vital to your self-discovery. Your response to people on all levels indicates something about yourself. Each individual that you have an experience with has been established with certain emotional, physical and spiritual components that are a part of the formula that you wish to gain from. They are aligned with the plan that you came with. They are a form of intelligence to you, and the way they relay that intelligence is the experience you have with them.

It's interesting to note the ways that you have used this intelligence when you look back on your interaction with people throughout your life! It is crucial to note that you have all chosen to be on Earth at a time where the energy is amplified in such a way that you are made more aware of the contrasts. This has accelerated your own ability to "know selves" and to realize the need to be accountable for your life.

You have also chosen to be on a planet where you have the choice of being in physical male or female bodies and are able to be involved in the human experience with its physical, emotional, mental and spiritual abilities. This choice has widened your capability of expression, therefore, giving you full authority to exercise the free will you have. There are many planets and dimensions that do not have the same level of expression that you have here, and so it seems rather a pity that so many here are born with so much to say, and yet they say so little. Your message to this world is your life. Though there is never any obligation to be something or do something, would you truly wish to live in a way limiting yourself when you know that you have the ability to always allow your whole being to sing?

You were never born to hurt, to feel pain in any way at all. Life was not set up as a battleground for the conflicts of mind and body, and it is, indeed, sad to see that human nature has at times turned life into a dangerous place internally and externally. You are as God and, therefore, your true nature is love, and from love comes light that offers unlimited ways of expressing that love and amplifying that life. Moving away from this energy of love establishes destructiveness, and yet even this energy has its purpose.

As you evolve through your lives, inevitably you are led to a new attentiveness and a desire to evolve through love and not through disparaging emotional and physical experiences. And yet how people still fight! This fight, this discord has all come about because they are not conscious of the light and, therefore, cannot see what they are creating. I often have defined enlightenment to mean to "be in light of life." There is always a point when you realize how much better life is when you live it with all the lights on. That would, indeed, stop you from stumbling around in the dark, bumbling into life and hurting yourself. If the lights are on, then you can see what you are dealing with.

Seeing allows you to know what you do not want, and it gives you the choice of where to position yourself. This is basic common sense. As you stop paying attention to what you are creating and stop being aware of your position, you became more unaware of what you are accumulating. At some point inescapably, you will be called upon to be accountable for your actions, or lack of them as the case may be! It may take several lifetimes to build up this pattern—or not. We are finding in our observations that you are willing to resolve the issues you have created sooner or later. This is an indication that human nature is understanding the patterns it is creating and wishes to remedy the situation sooner than later. And all will be on hand when it is needed, for the soul has an astonishing ability to recall anything it needs to [recall]—and often from the human nature's perspective at the most unsuitable times!

Your Soul Has an Astonishing Memory to Recall Anything It Needs.

The above statement is a truth. You, the soul, will never forget anything .It will take on all information, and it will use it to create other realities that you will then live out in order to keep evolving. You are wired for higher! Do you really think that you as God would ever accept being less than what you were created as?

This is why despite the fact that many people can plunge to the greatest depths of despair, ultimately they find a way of reaching up and know that up is where they should be. The program you all have within that says "Create more" kicks in and sends the appropriate messages to the human nature which understands the need to survive. Creation energy inspires survival energy to take big steps towards a different reality and a better outcome.

A Change of Scenery Changes the Vibration.

As the emotional scenery changes, there is a shift in the backdrop that represents the issues of your life and the way you are involved in these issues. As you raise your own awareness, you move away from the density and note a change in the temperature, so to speak. You find self-adapting to this lighter energy by making relevant changes. When events in life indicate that there are changes that you need to make, then you have reached a crucial point of change. You have to be careful that you do not stay locked in the same vibration that represented the "problem" if you actually already have moved away from it. It's rather like driving an automatic car. It shifts its gears as it "reads" the conditions. You are no different. You are the soul driving your body through life, and your soul has systems that shift the gears to fit the conditions of your life; however, when you look at what you're sharing the road of life with, it might pay to take a defensive driving course!

As you pull away from the situations that no longer serve you, this is the time where you need to be a more conscious observer and creator of your life. As you become stronger and more capable, you should take more notice of where you are going, what you are feeling, and how you are responding to what you are observing. This action triggers in the soul a process where the soul recalls happier and more balanced moments in life, and it uses this as a new reference point that helps it to find a new platform of stability. It may not be the exact answer it seeks, but it does give the human nature some sense of security to stand on, then build on, and move on.

Some people have said that they have changed everything, but the energy still feels the same. This indicates that they have changed the furniture and have a new look but have not actually shifted away from what was! When you evolve in life, you have to look at what you believe and at times change those beliefs in quite dramatic ways, and that means changing your life in dramatic ways. One also has to take what one believes and make it a way of living. Many keep separate what they believe and how they live, and this creates discrepancies leading to confusion. Even GOD is a way of living as opposed to a belief. When you truly make it a way of life, you get the full benefits of the energy!

CHAPTER THREE

We are the stuff that everything is made of.

Author Unknown

And so, we have this young boy growing up in Canada having an ever-growing sense of isolation and a sense that there was so much more about everything than what he could see— uncomfortable amongst his peers and feeling more able to communicate in the adult world but not knowing where he was to position himself. He was polite and gracious, and there was a definite shyness about him that was based on his uncertainty. He had a fear of getting it wrong and not wanting to be humiliated and yet at times would seek out experiences unconsciously and otherwise that would draw attention to him. He could be argumentative and liked to feel he knew better though he was not self-righteous.

And what made him happy? Peace, harmony, beauty, quiet and order, being alone and not having to deal with everyday things in life. He was tidy, and he liked being in a place where there was no conflict. Open spaces, cold crisp mornings and the smell of freshness, and the feeling of life waking up every morning. I'm beginning to sound like a verse out of "My Favourite Things" so I'd better stop whilst I'm ahead!

One thing that I felt very at ease with also was small compact spaces. My sister and I used to play "train compartments" in the closet of her bedroom that had sliding doors. We would set up chairs for the bunks and for hours would act out our game. We would also sneak from our kitchen our latest food craze at the time that was sugar mixed with raw oatmeal, ugh! I liked the darkness of the space, and it felt easy and protective. This contentedness of small places and darkness is with me to this day.

Also, I am convinced I have had several lifetimes as a nun as I have been fascinated by them all of my life, and I truly feel I "know" what it is like to be a nun and how it is for them. I am not talking about the modern nun of today, but those in full religious regalia of starched wimples, black serge, calico knickers and swinging crucifixes tied around the waist. There is one exacting image that is often in my thoughts and particularly presents itself to my conscious mind when I am feeling out of sorts. It is a young nun walking down a long cloister hallway with tiles of yellow and rust stretching down the expansive corridor. To the left is a square lawn and all feels safe with those safe and solid confines of stonewalls all around. There is always a sense of deep peace when this thought comes to me.

One of my favourite books has been *Through the Narrow Gate* written by an ex-nun Karen Armstrong who has gone on to be a well-known scholar and writer. I have literally read this book at least a hundred times and always take great comfort from reading her story because I "know" what it was like. I had been there. So the nun part of me is still in there somewhere, and at times brings back the old habits! Ok, I know that's bad, but come on, you can see that it had to be said!

I also know I have been a cook in a past life, and at some point in some old cavern of a kitchen in a stately home in England. To this day I can walk into anyone's kitchen and know my way around, feeling very at home and, of course, I love to cook. It feels like my territory. Whilst visiting old stately homes in Britain, I would always seek out the kitchens and have a good old poke around.

I believe that our life now is always throwing up opportunities to recall the other lives that we have led. We see this in the people that we bring into our lives and how we feel that we know them, by the cultures that we are drawn to, and the places that seem familiar to us. Past lives seem to return by the things we do and how we just seem to know how to do them! Some years ago I had a go at the sport fencing. A good friend who had fenced on an international level arranged for me to visit her club, so I presented myself and was duly kitted out.

The uniform felt so familiar to me, and I could literally feel my body adjusting to it, and the way I stood and walked just changed. When the teacher showed me the basic stance and some basic moves, I instantly went into the correct position and was all ready to take on the opponent! The teacher looked at me and commented that I must have studied before. I was thinking, "Well, not in this lifetime!" On another occasion my best mate organized a "boys' weekend" in the country: riding quad bikes and doing some skeet shooting. I had never held a rifle or any sort of gun in my hand, and yet when it came to shooting the skeets, I just naturally blasted them out of the sky!

When I look back now at my early years in Canada and with what I now know, I can see those other lives and how they were influencing the way I presented myself in life, and, of course, the way I viewed the world and people around me. Now it makes me think differently of the people that were in my life then and why I had positioned them there. One realizes that we are born master strategists, who all through our lives are positioning people and what they represent at certain strategic points. This tactic is inherent in us all, and despite whether we know it or not, we are all participating in it. I can look at that "little" Blair and see that he was this myriad assembly of thoughts and experiences that were all based on the choices he made, having drawn from the cornucopia of his many lifetimes. And I can now see and feel that on quite a big level, he knew that and was accepting of that. He was also frightened of that, as what he felt about himself didn't match up with the very big feeling of something great and grand and important.

He was thinking, "How could I fit little me into something that is so much?"

I think that is happening to us all now at this time in our history. Life on all levels is getting bigger, and with the way the God energy is presenting itself more obviously, it is making people look at how they fit into this new way of being. There seems to be a conflict of interest between the God part of us and our human nature part of us that is confusing the energy, as we are not who we were and people have to create something new. You cannot create the new by staying blatantly attached to the old energy, and I feel this is what a lot of us are doing. We have to truly detach from what was and focus on what is the new energy and, therefore, the new launching pad for the new way of living.

We are accessing more about life on new levels than we previously have, and the way we access this is simpler than what some of us have conceived. From my own personal observations and the ways I have participated in my life, I have come to see that we are accessing this new energy through the patterns of our day-to-day lives. There is a subtlety about the way that we are being shown this and because of the simplicity, we tend to miss it! I think many are waiting for some obvious sign or signal, some epiphany that will unexpectedly catapult us all into an evolved and enlightened state or at least give us some clear answers in how to adapt to all of this new way of being. As I write, this I get the image in my mind of a great finger pointing at humanity indicating that that's where you look!

That theory is pretty obvious, and the sense of responsibility for our own outcomes seems to be making itself more manifest through our day-to-day routines. So the answer is not *in* ourselves, the answer *is ourselves*. If we bring in the karmic deals that we have made and attach this theory to them, we see that we are involved in an energy that is perpetually us on all levels and that we are accessing this energy by how we participate in life. So this makes me think more about the people that I have positioned in my life, and I see them from a totally different perspective. I see that, in fact, they are simply *aspects of myself* that I have placed there and, of course, not just the people but all of my experiences, emotionally, mentally physically—and that concept rather changes the scenery! I am as we all are, in a constant state of seeing ourselves in our life and, therefore, living out all these selves through our response. As children we have vivid imaginations, conjuring up all sorts of information and stories that to adults are just our childhood fancies and games—but are we, in fact, simply accessing information from higher levels of ourselves and tapping into the collective energy of source energy? Are we also attuning in to the spirits and energy of beings that are there to give us comfort, assists us, and guide us through our lives?

Of the toys that I had as a child, the one I attended to the most was Fred. Fred was a little wooden figure no bigger than the size of a child's finger. I think he had been part of an old Noah's Ark set, and he had been one of the people. His bottom half was painted blue for his trousers, his upper half yellow for his shirt. The top of his head was beige; no doubt his cap or hair. He had little painted eyes and a nose, but for some reason, no mouth. Fred had an extraordinary life that, of course, I created for him. He had homes and holidays and fantastic jobs and relationships. I let my fantastical creative mind loose on Fred and his many adventures. He, indeed, had a very charmed and privileged existence. With all I created for him, I must have been drawing upon my own soul's experiences, and also perhaps this was a spirit guide's way of helping and teaching me to find expression? And what a wonderful way for spirit to guide, assist and comfort me in a non-frightening non-confrontational manner. And so Fred and I had this brilliant relationship. He was never one of those toys that you would tell everything to because it never felt appropriate to do so. I really loved Fred. He was lost to me somewhere in the move we made to New Zealand, but I hardly noticed as by that stage, Fred had served his purpose.

TABAASH SPEAKS

Deciding when you are to be born again is a very vital part of the advancement of your soul. History is a vibration, and you are history; therefore, all the vibrations of history are stories of souls whose choices not only evolved themselves, but the whole of consciousness. You may get a collective energy of souls who all choose to be born at a certain time of history where the events of that time will offer up colossal prospects for great advancement of human nature through the events that will occur. I cite the Great Wars of One and Two as prime examples of such occurrences. All the men and women who participated in these events made a choice to do so.

Every generation is attached to the collective frequency of that time, therefore, it is rather like a password that gives that generation access to life's information in a certain manner, and what this does is to enable that generation to evolve the previous one in thoughts words and deeds. I shall use music and Elvis and the Beatles as primary examples. The music that they presented to the world held for the youth of the day a vibration that was relevant to the place that generation felt they had in the world. It encompassed the new way of thinking and being and expressing life. Previous generations felt challenged and at times offended by what was being presented and tried unsuccessfully to boycott and repress what was happening. As they say though, you can't hinder progress! I suppose in a way all generations don't want to feel that the position they have is being usurped by the next.

Each generation brings with it a specific vibration that is exclusive to that generation. It is a collective group of souls who choose the time in history to be born into; with that choice they bring with them a vibration that will stimulate the energy of Earth in a particular way. That is why when you look back through history, there were certain events and changes that occurred with particular generations. This, of course, has had positive and negative effects on the comings and goings of human nature. Each soul who chooses to come into what I shall call "that Earth time" is actually linked in and influenced by the energy of every soul who is part of their team. At times there is a mass of souls who choose certain places to be while they are alive, so they can experience what is relevant to their evolution—hence, countries that are always in conflict, others where there is a major multi-cultural society, others in more exclusive settings where they seem unaware of what is happening in the world. Some choose heavily populated areas where there are social, political and economic discrepancies. The advent of mass communication has positioned everyone where they are more aware than ever about what is happening, and because of this, people are more conscious of the stories of the world. This exposure has a huge impact of the amount of awareness you all have and, therefore, this changes history. This also gives you access to more resource material so that in your awareness, you are able to improve your life in ways that are newly possible.

You Are All Great Reference Libraries.

So where you are and how you are in every way you can imagine is exactly where you have evolved to be. Your choices are no random acts. Anyone alive on Earth weighed all the repercussions of being alive at a time when everything is amplified in its contrasts. And being involved in the energy is actually amplifying you as well and, therefore, making you more conscious of who you are, what you think, etc. One may have heard of people saying that they must have been born at the wrong time, in the wrong body, and to the wrong parents, but this is simply not true. A soul at times will come into a new life with strong influences from other lifetimes or feel strongly that they feel related to a particular time in history. Regardless of the influences you have chosen to bring with you, you are alive now and this is your life!

The influences from other lifetimes are very relevant to the evolution of each individual and the population as a whole, but you must be careful to remember that you are the creator of everything and that you have access to all of source power and to not get caught up in what has been. What has been has served its purpose, and it took you to where you are. Where you are is your launching pad for "more" of you.

All of you have had lifetimes where your combined energy with another particular soul or souls has brought about positive and negative changes. In the field of medicine groups of souls have worked together to find cures and improve the physical well-being of people. In the world of politics and economics certain souls have come together to combine their energies to bring about positive changes. The world of arts, of course, is strewn with groups and duos whose performances have lifted the world in some way. In the field of science and warfare, think of all those who came together to bring the world into the nuclear age. Whoever they have been and whatever they were involved in, those souls concurred to participate in that experience.

So, do you ever get it wrong and live to regret your choices? Well, you may live to regret it in a human way, but the reality is that you *NEVER* make a wrong choice. If your life is showing indications that changes have to be made to avoid conflict, and you don't listen to you better judgement, then you still have made a choice. And consequently your life will be influenced by that choice.

Consider for a moment since the time of your birth just how much information that you have gathered and downloaded! Just as well, the soul is an unlimited source of power that is able to store up everything and have plenty of room for more!

You are in a Constant State of Preparation, Creation, Participation, and You Are living All of This Simultaneously.

At all times, physical or non-physical, your soul has access to all of life's information on both conscious and sub-conscious levels. Through your whole life, your soul will refer to this information to assist your human nature in its endeavours. The more you become conscious of self as God, the more aligned you are to its power, therefore, allowing you access to appropriate vibrations when needed. This accounts for times you have a feeling that everything will be ok or that you just have a sense of what to do. This was the soul going to the "library" and gathering the relevant information. In times of great distress and conflict, many have become aware of this "booster" that has given them a sense of courage and peace in the face of adversity.

Everyone does this, of course, regardless of the fact that they may have no conscious belief whatsoever spiritually. It's something that you were fitted with automatically when you were created, and it's in constant use! Most people would refer to this as intuition, perception, and the inner voice—that funny feeling that they know something. It is simply the God part of you doing the job, and it will always serve you even if you are not allowing it to on a conscious level. *Allowing* is a very important word here, as nothing can ever happen to you unless you allow it to happen. Your God-self knows exactly what you would permit, and that's why it keeps you linked into the file of free will and choice. So what actually occurs to your human nature when you make this connection with God on a more conscious level?

Everything about you is already programmed to be successful on all levels. When you stimulate the human nature with the God vibration, you begin to send information through you in a way that awakens your whole being into wanting to pull together. Imagine a still clear pool of water with you in the centre of it. Now imagine you have God's energy emanating from your heart chakra, and the energy begins to ripple out from the heart. This energy permeates your body and goes beyond, rippling outward further. In your consistent connection with God, you have this ripple effect continually occurring, and it's this consistency that trains your body to be aligned with vibrations that you could turn into higher ideas that have no limitations. And because your whole being is programmed to be in a state of unfailing wellness, this programme is activated, consequently giving you a complete state of awareness. This awareness becomes a platform of creation for you, and you will draw upon both physical and non-physical aspects of self to guide you to the best effort. Should you not be conscious of this awareness, you simply overcome the hurdles that you keep placing in front of you until you reach that awareness. This is not a complex process which one has to study for many years or lifetimes. One does not find it in the some sort of elite spiritual practice or group that sees themselves as the "enlightened ones." You are, all of you, this awareness and you are this *now*.

CHAPTER FOUR

What was is what was. Where you are now is what is.

Author Unknown

_____

In the northern summer of 1971, my parents made the momentous decision to move their family across the sea to New Zealand. Now here's some synchronicity for you—my fifth grade teacher was very interested in New Zealand personally and so during social studies we had studied that country. So there was my soul obviously preparing me for that step in my life! From the studies we made, there seemed to be an awful lot of sheep but not a lot of people. They called popsicles "ice blocks," there was a lot of water and beaches, and you drove on the other side of the road. All very useful information for an 11 year old!

Looking back now as I'm writing this, I can see how my higher self was simply preparing me for that next step in my life, and it reminds me of those choices we make before we are even born and how it allows us to fulfil the plan we have created. Of course, I was completely unaware of that way of thinking at the time and was simply following my parent's dreams and ideas of moving us far away from everything that we had ever known. With the decision made, we all got caught up in the wave of this new energy that suddenly permeated our young lives. All the excitement of putting the house on the market, the neighbourhood's curiosity when the sale sign went up on the front lawn, the feeling when the house had actually been sold that it's all really happening, saying goodbye to my father's white Pontiac Parisienne with the red leather upholstery. I recall vividly the people who had bought it—a young couple, the man with longish hair and sideburns, a blonde woman whom I told she was pretty and then blushed when she acknowledged it! They for some reason took the ironing board as well, which at the time I thought was a rather odd thing to do. Perhaps it was all part of the deal?

Before all of this selling and giving away of ironing boards, we did a trip to Alberta in the car to visit and say goodbye to various relations who lived from BC to Alberta. It was high summer and very hot. Dad had a big container of water that he had frozen, and so we stayed cool by drinking the icy water or sucking on the ice when it started to break up. It was a whirl of meeting up with people—some of whom I had never met before or seen since—a time of family dinners and bunking down with cousins. Hot prairie landscapes, and cool mountain ranger. Lakes and picnics, the laughter and anticipation, and, of course, my Dad's cousin and her breasts. We visited her family on our journey; I don't know where it was—such a jumble of places. We pulled up the drive and out of the house emerged this woman, clad in something soft and silky, black hair swept up all halo-like, smelling of something exotic—and two large glorious mounds of flesh pushed up high like some great mountain ranges that could rival the Rockies any day! She swept me into a huge embrace and clutched me to her ample bosoms. My face was pressed into folds of perfumed luxury, and, quite simply, I was lost.

All those people and all those souls that in my reality I had created. Years and years later when I understood that we all create the connections with everybody in our lives, it made me pay more attention to who was in my life, but it also made me think about why I had created some people to be specifically in my life while others were simply backdrop. Why were some people in our lives for five minutes while others were there for fifty years? Why do we start our lives someplace and grow up and then end them in another place? Why did I create my Dad's cousin? Was it just for her breasts?

Of course, all of these souls have a link with who we are. They represent aspects of ourselves. When the chemistry is there, we keep the formula of that connection alive, and when it's finished, we simply move on to the next formula. We are all each other, and we are continually looking for aspects of ourselves through the changing dynamics of the relationships we have with the world we live in and with each other. Even as children when our lives change because of the choices other people make, we have to understand that our own soul made that choice, and we simply aligned ourselves to the right people who would allow us to fulfil the choice you made. Our soul had it all mapped out, and as we become more aware of our God nature, it makes it so much easier to understand the life that we are constantly creating, and it gives more sense to the way that we have lived and are living our life.

Across the road from our house in Canada lived Sharon and Larry Burns. They had a small son called Brian and a baby daughter called Donna. As the baby grew into a toddler, she attached herself to me. She always wanted to be with me and cuddle me and was constantly drawn to my presence. She would curl up on my lap and lean her little head against me and look up at me with such love and devotion. I simply took it all in my stride and complied. Years on, I realized, of course, that she was recognizing me from some past life we had together. I wish I had known that then. How different our lives would be if we were all brought up knowing that we had lived before and that all the people we encounter in our lives are opportunities to evolve.

A few years back, I was out of town working, and I went into the lobby to meet up with my client. When we met, there was an instant feeling of knowing from both of us, and he actually had tears in his eyes. I gave him a hug and felt like I was hugging my long lost brother. In fact, we have become firm friends and when I am with him, I actually feel like he is my older brother and that I can lean on him and rely on him. All of our lives we are looking for these connections, and we should never miss the opportunity to further those associations when we are presented with them and our life. We want to keep on developing those links that through history have been so vital to our growth. And each time we link in again, we see it all from a different angle playing out a new and varied role.

During our trip to visit the relations, we visited great uncle Alex who was my father's uncle on his mother's side. I vaguely recall an old man in the garden, but it was what was in the garden that was far more fascinating. Life-size statues of dinosaurs filled the garden. This man was a brilliant artist and was also known for his hypnotherapy as I found out years later when my aunt sent me an old photo of him advertising his abilities. The picture is of him in his twenties or early thirties staring at the camera with a sort of demented psychical smile on his lips. Looking at this picture it would rather put you off rather than let him hypnotize you! I felt that he was a very spiritual man though and recall his gentleness.

And so we said our farewells to grandparents, aunts and uncles, cousins, friends and places and, in my case, my Dad's cousin and her perfumed breasts. We drove back to BC where we packed up the house and moved in with Aunt Alice and Uncle Cliff in their house in Surrey. I never got a chance to say goodbye to my friends from school or the mad women of the forest or the cemetery or the Reverend Harrison's dead daughter. Everything seemed to happen so quickly, and suddenly I had stepped away from that part of my life.

My father went to New Zealand first on the ship Orsova, which carried all our worldly goods, as well as my Father. It was a too dry day, and I remember well-being on the ship before it sailed. I felt awkward and suspended by all sorts of emotions I had never had before. We saw our trunks being loaded onto the ship, and I cried saying good-bye to my Dad, probably a mixture of all the emotions of the day and that fact that I loved my Dad deeply and would miss him. We drove to the shore near Stanley Park where we watched the ship sail out of Vancouver harbor till we could see it no more. It was a beautiful and sunny day.

It was September and the school year was starting, but we kids got an extended holiday. I wondered at the time what my friends thought when I wasn't there, or did they even give it a thought? My sister and I being so much older than the younger brothers decided that we should take their education in hand and so promptly appointed ourselves as their teachers, whether they liked it or not! We came to the agreement that we should have lessons everyday so no one would neglect the importance of education. Of course, this lasted all of five minutes once we discovered that our mother was not overtly concerned that we had this extended holiday, and so we abandoned our short careers as academics and instead whole heartedly dedicated ourselves to climbing numerous fruit trees, and, of course, eating the fruits that were in a large front lawn of our aunt and uncle's home. At the back, the garden was smaller, but there was long grass and you would often find red razor snakes and frogs there.

An old couple called the Shaws lived next door, Mrs. Shaw was a tiny groomed grandmotherly woman who had snow-white hair, worn up, and Mr. Shaw was a quiet gentleman to the core. This tender couple would often come to dinner, and when they did, you felt that you wanted to be quiet, sit still and mind your manners!

I liked them very much and with the sensitivity that children have, I was aware of their agedness and felt loving and protective around them. Everything about them from the way they felt to the way they smelled brought out in me a deep respect for who they were and for the life that they lived. I have always felt great respect for my elders and possessed the need to nurture them and help them maintain their dignity. In the presence of elder men, I always felt the need to call them "sir," as opposed to their name, something must have been instilled in me from other lives!

Those last months in Canada seemed a very "in-between time"—sleeping in sleeping bags on army stretchers in the basement.

"Why did I always get the old sleeping bag that smelt musty and had a large rip in it?" I'd ask.

"Because you are the eldest boy."

"Well, THAT never made any sense to me at all!" I pondered in frustration.

Then there was over-feeding the tropical fish in the small dark room downstairs—which to me seemed mysterious and full of intrigue. It never occurred to me what my mother must have been feeling or thinking moving her family to the other side of the world away from her own family and everything that she knew.

We sometimes would visit her mother, Nana, at White Rock Beach where she lived in a small flat in a very large old house on a hill. More days filled with sun and sand, the smell of fish and chips and train oil as the train tracks ran along the coast and, therefore, near the beach. We would at times put pennies on the track so the train would run over them and flatten them, and eat ice creams, my favourite being liquorice with its dismal grey colour, take long walks, climbing up and down the steep wooden steps that would take us back to Nana's place and back again to the beach. We were always told not to climb the rocks on the beach too much as we might fall and cut ourselves. I slotted that into the same file as "Don't go into the forest" and, therefore, proceeded to not only climb as many as possible but also picture in my mind the gruesome and bloody injuries one would attain from these dangerous rocks.

One day we heard the sound of an ambulance shrieking up the road. Of course, ambulances had the same fascination for me as hearses did. My mind went riot with pictures of limbs that were torn and mangled, decapitated heads, screaming patients writhing in agony amongst blood-soaked sheets. The fact that the ambulances of the day had curtains on the window fuelled my curiosity, so that always made me wonder what they were hiding. What macabre and disgusting sights was I being denied?

Once on a family drive we passed an accident and as the traffic slowed, I was in the fortunate position at last to see the "victim." She was unconscious and leaning against the side of the window; a little trickle of blood was coming from her mouth. I remember that she looked peaceful and had a small smile on her face. It never occurred to me that she might actually be dead. Perhaps she was? It would have been a bonus if I had known— at last a real dead body!

I wondered where she was while she was unconscious or perhaps dead. Again I had the feeling she was at the place where there was more and that place was wonderful.

Of course, all the holidays had to come to an end by then, and so in late September of 1971 the day finally came for us to leave Canada and embark on our new life in New Zealand. We were all kitted out in special outfits for the journey as people still dressed up for international air travel then. I had white and red striped bell bottomed trousers and boot shoes, as I called them. I was most insistent on having them and when we went to the shop to buy them, I tried as best I could to explain to the salesman. He went into the back and took absolutely ages, and then when he came back he was carrying a pair of large leather workman's boots with steel capped toes! The look on my face said it all.

My mother went and had her hair "done," and this amplified the importance of the journey as one only had one's hair "done" for something really special. The only things I really remember when we left were at the airport: my Nana standing there looking very vulnerable and trying hard not to cry, my adored Aunt Beverly bawling her eyes out, Uncle Cliff and Aunt Alice looking sad but no doubt feeling relieved that they would have their house back to themselves and back to being child-free and quiet! I felt quite solemn and grownup and took it all in my stride.

We flew aboard Air Canada to Hawaii and took an Air New Zealand DC 8 to Auckland where we were to live. As I stated, it was still quite special to fly offshore, and there was real china to eat off and real cutlery as well. The food was wonderful and the seats were roomy. We were given hot towels that smelled of the cologne 4711, and to this day whenever I smell that, I am transported back to September 1971. We kids, of course, fought over who would get the window seat, but Mum had a system worked out so we swapped every few hours, so we all had good window time. Sitting up there in the sky, looking out at the puffy white clouds, I felt closer to my something more.

The stop in Hawaii was short and only a day, but we had a hotel room on the beach where we could rest and refresh. Not that we spent much time doing that! We walked around Waikiki most of the day marvelling at the shops and beaches and the palm trees. There was lunch in a restaurant where I ordered shrimps that came served in a big hollowed out pineapple. Late afternoon found us back at the airport taking us closer to our destination. We arrived in Auckland early in the morning, and there was my wonderful Dad, waiting to sweep up his family in his arms. He piled us into a blue Toyota wagon (rented), and we drove into our new future.

In 1971 Auckland was not the developed and cosmopolitan city that it is today. The drive through Mangere, where the airport was situated, was a drive through the country. No shops, buildings, industrial areas—just fields, and water and sheep and cows. All I had expected actually. Our first house in Auckland was farmland, and beaches surrounded 5 Challinor St in a new subdivision called Pakuranga. It. It was the most idyllic of setting for children and adults alike. Our new home had a small front lawn and a large back section. There was a big garage that could easily have housed three cars; there was a playhouse and kiwifruit and passionfruit vines, as well as lemon and grapefruit trees! There was constant sunshine and the feeling of peace.

One of my first memories of our new house and life was the smell of a disinfectant called Dettol. It pervaded the house, and isn't it funny when I smell that smell now, it actually brings a tear to my eye. There were three bedrooms so the boys shared one room, and the other for my sister and my parents. After settling in, Dad took us all out to dinner in the city. I felt all dizzy and wobbly, and though it was not unpleasant, I couldn't figure out why I felt like I was going up and down and elevator. Dad said it was "jetlag" and, of course, I felt very important as no one else had it. HA!

Dad had enrolled us in the local school called Anchorage Park that was a handy five-minute walk from home. And so the day after we arrived in New Zealand, we went back to school. This was not a good experience for me as I was totally shocked and unprepared for the school. It was made up of a cluster of prefabricated buildings scattered amongst what seemed to be a field. These buildings had noisy wooden floors and windows that rattled. There was no heating. There was a small section of quite modern-looking buildings, three in a row that actually looked like a school, which was for the senior pupils. All the boys wore shorts and short-sleeved shirts and most of them were barefoot. There was a school dental nurse and dental clinic which was aptly named the murder house no doubt due to the fact that the drill she used was a foot pumped apparatus that looked like it came from the torture chamber of the inquisition!

My first classroom experience was just as shocking to me. Wooden desks with inkwells, and the lids of the desks lifted up, and the floor was all dusty and dirty. No polished linoleum there! The teacher came into the room and told us all to put hands on our heads. What did she think we were going to do, play with ourselves? All of this was most perplexing, and I can't say I went home full of the joy of new things. I felt really uneasy, and the local kids approached me with energy of curiosity blended with hostility.

My guard was instantly up and once again I felt myself being defensive, which always gave me an air of being reserved, and I suppose to some they saw this as arrogance. It was fear though, fear of being different now in this new world. I adapted in the ways that I always had done when I felt this—I kept to myself. Big mistake! Within a month of starting school, it seemed I had become public enemy number one, and so from that time to when I finished high school, it was like that. I was too different, too much the foreigner, too reserved, too weird for some. Nice little challenge as a soul I had set myself. The dye had been cast though, and there was no getting away from what I had been plunged into.

It wasn't like it was a constant battle, I did make friends and explored and fitted in the best way I could, but there were the occasional battles with other boys who thought me strange. I should have thrown myself completely into it all, but I had no idea what the rules were, and there seemed to be no one around to teach me. I let the fear get the better of me, and, therefore, in the process ostracized myself. Yet when I did get it right, people seemed uncomfortable around me and didn't know how to be with me.

We adapted to our new life in New Zealand, and I have to admit that I am grateful for the decision my parents made to move all those years ago. It was an idyllic country that at the time was not blatantly influenced by other countries and their issues. Milk was 2 cents a pint, and you could feed a family of six very well on very little. There was always sunshine and a simplicity that was refreshing and inspiring. There was not the feeling of survival that you get in bigger countries with bigger populations. Instead, there was more time for actual living. There was a naïveté and lack of sophistication, and equality amongst the Kiwis. People really did look out for each other, and it was safe and clean and green. The pace of life was relaxed, and it gave you an opportunity to really feel and observe what was going on around you. There was only one television station, and it started late in the morning and finished long before midnight. Dad decided not to get a television so we read more books and listened to the radio. We developed ourselves in a way that we probably never would have had we stayed in Canada. The move was a great gift as I see it, and I feel very fortunate to have grown up in such a way with such advantages.

I was enrolled in the Buckland's beach Sea Scouts where I learned to sail and row and go on long camps over the summer on isolated islands, surrounded by the glorious South Pacific Ocean. Dormant volcanoes were dotted all over Auckland, and we made many excursions to these, climbing down the now grassy slopes of the craters, exploring and wondering. On some of those Sea Scout camps we usually ended up camping on some farmer's land, which inevitably ended up with "we scouts" cutting down scrub on the land we were camping on. Obviously a deal had been struck with the landowner: you camp, you clear what seemed like a million hectares of scrub, and we will do the best to exploit this cheap labour!

Personally, I felt that we had the raw end of the deal, and I'm sure that we were very close to transfiguring into land scouts, as there seemed to be a very strong lack of sea connection. I also recall the latrines that we had to dig ourselves. They were so disgusting, and there was NO WAY I was going to do my business in them—thank you very much. Surrounded by bits of sacking that gave a very poor impression of privacy, abuzz with a gazillion blow flies, it was so vile, and I was too self-conscious about squatting down on that deep dark hole full of, well, you know. So the first few days I managed quite well and became quite used to my constipation. Nature really did have to take its course though, and so I would go on midnight crap excursions when no one knew. Ah, the relief of it all!

TABAASH SPEAKS

There are many moments in life where you become conscious of a new level of knowing. This knowing has always existed, but it is a knowing that has nothing to do with your human nature but all to do with your God nature. To access this knowing, you must awaken to a level that constitutes your conscious God nature, and by doing this, you awaken to the reality that there is something more to pay attention to and work with.

Let's put this question to you: *What must it feel like to be God?*

Sit quietly and allow yourself to relax and pay attention to the idea that you simply exist. You are in a room, you breathe, you feel, and you have awareness of life on many levels all at the same time.

This awareness is made up not only of the physical sense that you possess but the senses of the soul that will take your perception of life beyond the realms of all that is physical and emotional and mental. The more you relax, the more you are less aware of your body and more aware of yourself as soul, and through soul, you have altered your state of consciousness to another level of where you also exist. You are paying attention now to another part of you and, therefore, heightened your awareness to a place that up to that point you may have been unaware of. Your attention is now on that aspect of you. You are peaceful, you are clear, and you feel you sense more about you and beyond you. As you contemplate this feeling you are moving into the domain of the creator energy. As peace enfolds you, you sense that you truly do exist further than what your body has experienced, and you know that you are always living as the source of life. You may feel like you simply *are* life.

God is not a belief or a person but more the highest state of consciousness that can exist. It is source power that feeds upon itself, creating a force that pulses and expands. As it does so, it creates more of the source by doing this. As this energy is pulled together, it gathers into a dense mass of energy that compresses and compresses until it eventually has to expand. This expansion is an explosion of light frequency that reaches out as far as it chooses to go and then ripples right back to where it began—a pulsing, expanding, magnetic force that is the consciousness that is known as God.

This Is the Stuff That Everything Is Made Of.

This Is What It Feels Like to Be God.

And this is why you are, and all is considered to be God. You are this very energy, not just your soul but also everything that exists about you and all you represent in mind and body.

This God formula is endemic throughout this universe and beyond. One could say that this is the formula that makes life. The consistent pulsing and expanding ultimately moulds the energy into forms of expression that from the point of human science become the physiology of matter. As the matter is created, it begins to assert its own power over itself and organises itself into a position of alignment that is in harmony with other formulas that it is attracted to. It is able to do this because it is simply an extension of the God source and, therefore, carries exactly the same vibration and ability that the God force has. It can align itself to similar vibrations, therefore, attaching itself to these. This manifests as larger forms of energy being created. As these energies form, they store massive amounts of energy and create a huge magnetism that keeps pulling in more energy.

What Becomes of This Energy?

This energy becomes the stars and the planets; it becomes the universes and the all that is in the universes. It's all dimensions; it is all forms of life in fact that exist in all-possible structures. That energy is also all souls and all the expressions that the souls participate in, be it physical or non-physical. The advent of your soul was your very birth of consciousness—you as God extending yourself to find greater expression from the diverse opportunities that in which you participate. It is important to bring up here that your soul is not a human soul, but the pure energy of God and consequently you are able to find expression in all of life's experiences on Earth and all that lies beyond.

The implications of this are, of course, quite interesting as now you realize that you are a total infinite source of power that has no boundaries and an enormous amount of clout! So in terms of living on Earth, what are the implications? It means that all souls experience all forms of life. It is that you have not only been in human bodies but also have incarnate as everything that makes up this world. You have been the mountains and the seas and lakes and rivers; you have been animal and vegetable. You have been all forms of life on this planet. And the power of God, this pulsating force of energy is you, and it allows you to be alive and live out your experiences. It is found between matter, and it unites you all as a collective consciousness. It's this collectiveness that you feed from, and it gives to you the information that you require to be alive and to create your life. This is the force that attracts you all to each other—not the fact that you have lived before and built up karma.

This Is You Being God.

The access to this power, unremitting as is the power itself, can never be lessened or destroyed. It can only expand and find a greater level of expression. This is what you are, and this is what human nature is discovering at this time in history. You are discovering this, and consequently it is changing your life and changing the collective patterns of belief that human nature has been engaged in.

Imagine now for a moment that your soul is like a giant CD that goes off out into infinity. The middle of the CD is your body, accessing information from that part of your soul. That part of your soul has information that you yourself are permitted to access, and you access this information, based on the belief systems that you are driving your life form. What you access is feeding your belief and, therefore, will validate what you know and the way that you are living this life. This information will affect your mind, body and spirit beliefs.

You have chosen to be incarnate on Earth, and you have made specific emotional agreements that define what sort of information you allow self to attain in this life. With these agreements in hand, so to speak, you are born, and you begin to involve yourself in your life, based on all the agreements you have created. When you look at the makeup of a CD, it has information that has been burned onto it. A laser light plays over the information; hence, you are able to listen to whatever information is on the disc. Your soul has everything burned onto it as well, and so when you allow light to scan over your soul, you also have the ability to access the gathered information of life. Like a CD you also carry tracks that give you specific data that is pertinent to your needs; they are like other selves that you can access that carry this data. These other selves are possibilities in your life, and the ones that you attract to you are entirely based on what you are doing in your present.

It Is Literally Impossible to Attract Anything You Do Not Want.

All that is your life now is based exclusively on what you are permitting. When you become more involved in the development of the self, you begin to, as God does, expand your consciousness to attain more of what you wish, and this gives you right of entry to other levels of life. So to get what your whole being desires, you need to be specific in what your intentions are, and register these intentions by making them a way of life. Doing this establishes a relationship with the energy of the desired energy, and you begin to pull this energy in. You must be certain in your own energy and not be distracted by the past events or future possibilities.

You will begin to feel this energy, and with this feeling, you will attach ideas that you will then live out. Your instinctive self tends to kick in here, and it recognizes the higher energy that you have attracted, and it guides you through your instincts. The more confident you become in this, the easier it is to attract what you wish. A synchronicity tends to occur here as you are in an alignment with all the forces that you need. This is showing you that you are now receiving guidance from your own higher nature, which is helping you to see what it is that you need to do to ensure you get the best results!

Since You Exist Everywhere, You Have Access to Everything.

When It All Goes Wrong

When you have an erroneous alignment with the life forces that you are working with, you are not able to attract to you what you wish, and as a result, things will tend to not go your way. Several factors could be taken into consideration here: 1) your intent was not made clear or your thoughts, words and deeds; or 2) you are not at peace with your body and are not basing your intentions from a place of harmony but from the idea that you are a victim in conflict with life.

Over the years I have consulted with people who have been brought up in an emotionally abusive environment. The parents have consistently bombarded these people all through their childhood with derision and disapproval and berated them at every possible moment. This has left these people feeling wounded and scarred emotionally. As these people grew up and moved into their lives, they established certain belief systems around their childhood and themselves. They also forged negative ideas about parents and authoritative people, therefore, making it difficult for them to trust others or take guidance from those who would want to help.

As these patterns permeated their lives, they established a belief system that became a magnet for attracting the same situations throughout their lives. The energy of the belief system went out there and found ways of replicating what they were thinking and feeling and the ways they were participating in life. Aspects of them that fitted the profile they had established began to emerge and influence their lives in all ways. They simply created what was familiar to them.

Whatever You Pay Attention To Becomes Your Life.

Inevitably these people reached points in their lives where they could no longer sustain the pressure of living in such emotionally-charged negative ways. At times it inexorably took some to the edge, and they endured a major breakdown that led them back to the very foundations of themselves and their pain. Many people I'm sure can relate to this. At times the pain can manifest as a physical illness forcing the person to question the effectiveness of repressing unresolved feelings and ideas. I recall a client who was filled with such repressed anger that he had created benign tumours in his body. He hadn't a notion of what was causing these.

When he came to see me, the first thing I mentioned having greeted him was, "Who are you so angry with?"

He stared at me for a long while and then in a barely audible whisper replied, "My ex-wife.

You could almost see the anger rippling through his body, gathering all that negative energy.

I then told him that it was this anger that was the cause of his health issues and that to be totally healed from this, he had to forgive her. He looked at me in desperation and then said, "But if I do that, she has won."

I told him that she would surely win if he were to die from this. You see at this point the anger had only created *benign* tumours; there was always a chance that he could take it all a step further and manifest the situation as something more terminal.

He listened very carefully to my words and grasped the reality of what the situation was for him and what he was actually creating.

To his credit, he forgave her, and this created an interesting positive ripple effect onto not only his life but also the lives of his ex-wife and others. He was a wealthy man and his wife had been playing away with a man who was also wealthy. She left her husband for this other man and took half his wealth with her, despite the fact she had her own wealth. This had put this man to huge disadvantage for some time, and it had taken him a great deal of effort and hard work to once again get his head above water. When he contacted his ex and spoke of his forgiveness, it opened up many more doors of conversation for the two of them, and she began to do some soul-searching of her own. The end result was that she gave him back the money she had taken from them, and even more amazing was that the man suggested to his wife that they use that money to establish a charitable trust that assists young people who were disadvantaged.

This is a superb outcome to what had been and could have been more destructive. Of course, it does not always end up this way. Too often the results can be fatal on many levels as people hold onto their anger and pride, allowing their egos to keep finding ways of being revengeful and destructive at whatever cost. The result of this is not only the destructiveness of their current lives but also their other future lifetimes.

You Are Made Up of Many Selves

Since you are made up of many selves; it is important to know how to access these selves so that you are able to transcend selves that are counterproductive in your life. Now a point I wish to make here is that there is no such thing as a "bad self." There are productive selves, and there are counterproductive selves. The selves you attract are defined by the energy/ies you are paying attention to. You all have the ability to access whatever self or selves are relevant to you, and you do not have to have a master's degree in metaphysics to do so!

When awakening in the morning, consider for a moment the structure of your day. Which selves do you believe would be useful for you? I believe that you should all begin the day with the thought, "*I am God.*"

This is affirming your connection with the power source on a conscious level. Having done this considers your day and its events and simply calls in the aspects of self that are important. On a normal working week, you would call in your work self, your communication self, etc. For those who go to the gym, always call in your super human athletic self! The picture becomes much clearer as you affirm this, and it's so very easy.

Most people know the structure of the day and what they have planned, so this should not be too arduous a task. Practicing this also is training your leadership skills over your body and mind. As you build the energy of this structure, the mind and body components recognize what you are doing, and they understand the advantages to such leadership. As you institute this energy consciously through your life, you once again have that all-important alignment that is so fundamental to your survival.

Perhaps an easy thing to do would be to make a list of what you consider to be some *basic selves* that are imperative to your essential needs. Here are some suggestions:

- My health and well-being self;
- My peaceful and happy self;
- My prosperous self;
- My business self;
- My perfect relationship self;
- My God self.

Of course, the list is interminable as you find more and more of what you are and create more selves that you are able to work with. Using this method also makes you feel that you do have choice, and you are the one who is always doing the driving. This method is tremendously beneficial for those who carry experiences that have been shaping their lives in counter-productive ways. One could call upon the self that is at peace with an abusive parent or a bad relationship. This presents a new angle on how to address your old former conditioning.

Think about some of the everyday tasks that people have to be involved in throughout a basic day and yet see them as a waste of time because they would rather be doing something more productive or fun. So why not call in the selves that deal with these things in a more prosperous and patient way. Call in the housework self, the washing self, and the grocery shopping self.

All the files are out there, and it's up to you what you call up and how to use them!

When You Get It Right

When it's right, it is astonishingly, astoundingly, breathtakingly stunning! What could be greater than discovering that you are the ultimate architect of your very own existence, and that there is essentially no other way? You are always perfect, healthy, happy, creative, expressive and abundant, and you are also for eternity in harmony with all of life's forces. It is the ultimate and the definitive nirvana of existence that we all know. When you develop and live this belief you live by your God nature and realize that you strayed into the part of the garden of life that was always in the shade. It's like a recipe really. When one has the correct ingredients in the correct proportion and follows the recipe directions, the result is mouth-watering in contrast with the human phrase, "It tastes like a dog's breakfast!"

All souls know that life is all about harmony. That is why they seek out the something better that they believe exists and they deserve. The soul knows what is real and what is not, and it will remind you through your life that you have all these other aspects of self to draw upon and use. Despite some of the awful circumstances that you can find yourself in, your soul will remind you to evolve your beliefs and change your mind, body, spirit climate.

When the Climate Changes, You Have to Wear Something Different.

When you are involved in a relationship with God, all your selves resonate to that perfect vibration. Perfection is what you were created as, and it is your forever task to keep perfecting the perfect! In this state there is no more call to attract any occurrence that would necessitate discord in your life, which would only lead to more inconsistencies. Imagine no more relationship issues, no more financial burdens and worries, no ill health, nothing that would attract dissonance. You would have it all, you are it all, and you know that you create it all from the most celestial energy that is possible.

As people live this way, they must make certain that they evolve the way they have been living and also evolve the belief systems they have held onto for so long. People can read all the books and do all the meditations, do the courses, chant till they are hoarse, and stare into crystals till they are cross-eyed, and yet they don't seem to progress. It makes sense that as you evolve in one way, you have to inform all the other parts of your makeup that you've made some changes. Don't assume that all aspects will simply step into line. Remember they need that leadership from your ultimate self.

Those old emotional patterns can be very destructive if you don't evolve beyond them. It's like a great pile of rotting garbage full of the vilest things you could imagine. You can fool yourself for a while shifting the energy from place to place and give yourself the impression that you have dealt with it or changed something, but like rotting garbage, the stench becomes stronger and you can't ignore it. Unfortunately human nature has the proclivity to turn what could have been managed into human disease. You leave something rotten long enough, and it becomes a haven for something far worse. And goodness knows that at this time in history the last thing humans need is more garbage. Never before has the statement "Take out the garbage" been more relevant. On Earth people often talk about having faith and trust and the necessity of those energies. And yet when they do practice this, they seek for revelations beyond themselves because that is where they believe is where they will find the answers or make it all right.

There is nothing that can ever make it right for you; there is no one that can make it right for you. Only *you* live your life, have your thoughts and only you attract what you have. You really are the only one that has any influence over you. Whatever is available to you only comes to you because it is what you have permitted to allow to happen. You are the very revelation that you seek. For all beings, your vibration is a field of potential, and you are all in the process of casting off the old ways you have identified yourself with—old ways that are so draconian as to render them completely ineffectual in this time of light and harmony.

And yet some will stick to the old ways that seem comfortable to them. Human nature seems to have become addicted to the idea of conflict and embraces it, regardless of the injurious effects it has on life. Some believe that conflict is a part of life. It seems quite an undertaking to change when the climate is different. Yet inexorably you do, but you can make these changes without having to endure the unnecessary infringements you places on yourself.

CHAPTER FIVE

What? Return to Earth again? Is this some sort of joke?

Author Unknown

My spiritual growth during those years was through organized religion. We went to a local Anglican church in Panmure, Auckland called St. Mathias. It was a lovely small historic church built on a hill overlooking the Panmure basin, which was an extinct volcanic crater. It was an exquisite church with its wooden high-arched ceiling and quiet solitude. There were large oak trees all along the fence line on the right and the church graveyard on the left as you drove up. I never got the same feeling from that graveyard as I did from others. Most of the graves were quite old and some historic, so I'm pretty sure those spirits had certainly moved on!

I became an altar boy in this church and wore a red cassock and a white surplus, and as I carried the cross up the aisle, I tried my very best to look all holy and angelic and took my job to administering to the minister during Holy Communion very seriously! This worked a treat actually with some of the old ladies—as I soon found out to my advantage, as they would often press a crisp two-dollar note into my hand after service. From then on, I would practice sweet and butter-wouldn't-melt-in-your-mouth cherubic expressions to keep the coffers full. This worked rather well actually, and I could make quite a killing on special service Sundays when the church was packed to the rafters with gentle old ladies with full purses. And seeing that there were no other altar boys, I had no rivals to contend for the booty!

I loved going to the church early before service, as I would sit alone and feel the peace and solitude that the church offered me. The morning sun would cast coloured shadows onto the stone floor and the polished wooden pews, playing out a sort of spiritual dance. You could hear the birds chirping in the nearby trees. I used to think of all the people over the decades that would have sat in the pews and talked to God in their own ways. It felt like it was a sacred place in those quiet moments before the congregation arrived, and I feasted in the energy of that sacredness. Then it was back to business as I could hear the Reverend arriving, and I busied myself, getting everything tip top for the morning.

One of my greatest challenges during these services was when my mother would bring my little brother to the service. I would sit in my pulpit seat, not daring to catch his eye, as he would sit there simply staring at me with the blankest expression he could find. He knew exactly what he was doing, and it was a real challenge to suppress the laughter that wanted to erupt from me. In the midst of the most holy of sermons, catechisms, creeds and all those schisms for that matter, I had to call upon all the angels of paradise and beyond to help me. It was like trying to hold in a massive fart and all the discomfort and facial expressions that went with it! He never managed to crack me though my little brother gave it all his worth, and so I have to give him undue credit for his perseverance. Of course, this could work the other way as well.

There were times when I would sit up there looking all pious and serious and stare him down till he would get a fit of giggles, and my mother would be glaring at him with me remaining stoic and as Godlike as I could muster.

One Sunday as the Reverend and I were going up the stairs from the vestry into the church, we came upon the verger administering CPR to one of the elder females of the congregation who had suffered a cardiac arrest. I looked up at the Vicar, and he looked quite shocked, and the verger had such a look of distress on his face as he tried so hard to pump life back into this woman. As we passed and carried on with the service, I remembered that her name was Mrs. White, and that day in church, she died.

NOW! I thought of all the places that you can die, and this has GOT TO BE THE PLACE! I mean church, fast ticket to heaven and all that. My imagination by this stage was running riot.

There was a big folding door that separated the church from the area that led to the church hall, and that's where the body of Mrs. White lay through the whole service. This door had been closed, of course, but it was a complete magnet to me and through the service I tried to pierce the folding door with my eyes as behind that door at last was an actual BODY, and it was DEAD, and there was the strong possibility that on the way back to the vestry, I would actually SEE the BODY under the SHEET!

I was so excited and could hardly keep my mind on what I was supposed to be doing. The service seemed to go on and on and on, and then suddenly it was over and instead of my usual slow holy gait with the Vicar behind me, I broke into a rather unholy trot that could have rivalled any Olympic runner; the vicar was behind me trying to catch up. As I reached the folding doors, I was suddenly ushered out a side door I had never seen open before and was moved briskly away from "that place." I felt like I had been robbed. I did have a peak though under the gap of the folding door once I was in the hall and had a good view of the SHEET!

As I was getting out of my robes I could not help but think, here was this old lady who that morning had gotten up to go to church as she always did on Sunday, and that on some level she decided that it was time for her to go home to spirit, and she would never go back to her home ever again. Had she planned a Sunday roast? Was there washing on the line that needed taking in? What of her family and friends and her car, which was still parked outside?

As I passed the place where her body still lay, I stopped for a moment and tried to feel the energy. I felt peace and even though that peace and quiet was always there, an even deeper sense of sacredness seemed to pervade the room. Something had descended on that room. A door to God had opened, and she had gone home and maybe, just maybe, that door to God had been left a little open so that the rest of us could have a glimpse into that something more that we all knew existed. I was given a glimpse that day through that door, and it sowed something in me that was a foundation for my own spiritual future.

Being around the energy of death is a reminder to us all that there is something beyond what we know as life, and yet so many people are so afraid of death and dying. If we can all accept that there is always going to be that something more and know that it is a step into a life more unlimited, then we can all look differently at the way we live our lives whilst in the body. I suppose a lot of people who think that a young child with such a fascination with death was quite morbid. It wasn't really about death though; it was more about the fact that my soul was remembering spirit, and the energy of death triggered in me some deep knowledge of life beyond the body.

About two weeks after Mrs. White passed away, I was weeding the graves, and I saw a new grave, and it was Mrs. White's. A mound of earth piled high, rotting flowers and all around it, the noises of everyday life simply carried on without Mrs. White.

In that church I was confirmed and took my first Holy Communion. In that church I experienced the energy of death close-up. In that church I did some growing up and in that church I learned to hate the music of Cat Stevens as at the youth club I attended there was a guy who was obsessed with Cat Stevens' music, and he would play it incessantly!

In that church I did feel somehow that God was speaking to me but wasn't sure what it was all about. My mother would often say that I would make a good minister, but I knew that whatever God wanted me to do, that was not my calling.

TABAASH SPEAKS

You have probably notice that yes, you have done it again. You have been reborn, and you are back on good old planet Earth. For some of you this seems to be quite a habit, and for others of you, it may be a relatively new experience. It's still your choice though, and it is always yours and is never in the hands of any other source of energy. Have a really good look around you right now.

This is what you have created so far.
This all started with you.
This all began based on what you believed in.
This place you are in is a launching pad for more.
This is all your own choice.

I CHOOSE TO TAKE RESPONSIBILITY FOR WHAT I HAVE CREATED.

Inexorably all souls will come to the conclusion that it's just not worth the effort to fight and resist and punish themselves and others in the process of working out the life they live. Being accountable for everything you have created is not as easy task, and the struggle is enormous for some. Layer upon layer of old energies vying for space and your attention puts a gargantuan amount of pressure on you, and the results of that can so often be calamitous. Let's go through the points that I have made.

This Is What You Have Created So Far.

All your feelings, thoughts, actions have come from the way that you have *behaved,* and the way that you behaved is because of what you were paying attention to. This led you to creating a *belief,* and the consequences of all this is before you right now in your life. Do not be mistaken that this is some sort of mistake; you have exactly what you have created. You did not get off at the wrong stop, and you are not living the wrong life or at the wrong time or in the wrong body. You are attached to a specific energy line that has benefits for you, and the sooner you see this and instigate this in your life, the sooner you will benefit from this. These energy lines are created by you and are your thoughts and emotions and experiences that have come from all you have lived in this and any other life in whatever form you have taken. Imagine a fibre optic cable that is made up of hundreds, if not thousands of smaller, cables all massed together. Each smaller cable is a different colour that defines its vibration. All the cables work in harmony, and they are organized by you to do so. As you progress in life, you link into other networks, that is, basically everything else. These links transmit new pictures of possibilities to you, thus, allowing you to be a viewer of your own creation.

This All Started with You.

A crucial point to make here is that it's important that you do not get tangled up in some of the other links that are floating around. If this happens, that's when you "short circuit" which leaves you unable to function as a clear transmitter or to recover information you need in the clearest way. You can create static through your own energy lines and consequently send messages of confusion that jam everything up. Then, like a computer, it crashes.

So your original beliefs created the energy lines that you are currently connected to. If you are established at the beginning of your day from the highest point possible, then you have the best link that attunes you to the highest source of energy. Imagine this is like a *soul vitamin* that you need to take before you actually get out of bed! With the nutrition from this vitamin, you are fired up to be the ultimate creator of the day in front of you. So, remember to take your soul vitamin every morning!

You Are All Getting a First-hand Experience of the Power of Being God.

Nothing about where you are in your life is a chance act. There is no such thing as a wrong turn; if you feel you have taken one, it is because you have not been following the directions accurately. And if that is what you have done, then that is what you believed. This new energy that you are all now aligning yourselves to be is, in fact, excellent creative energy. It's on-call to everyone, and there is no complicated way that you have to attain this.

It's very essential to take advantage of the idea of this creative power since, after all, you are in the process of creating life every day at every point. How exciting to think that you are all witnesses to creation in a way that no other past generations on Earth have ever been. You are all getting first-hand experience of the power of God through the actual living of what you are doing, and you are able now be conscious of this should you choose to allow this to happen.

The total power of what I shall call *creation energy* is ubiquitous in all life now on an extreme and conscious level. This power, of course, has always been prevalent throughout history, but past generations on a collective level did not have the same awareness that is found today. In the past the energy was more survival and establishing and caught up in human nature and its experiences. God and source power were something that one had to worship rather than *be*. With the advent of the development of source power as a part of life, this energy is now being used for living and expanding this living through new ways of thinking and feeling and participating in life. It is putting *God Energy* into practice.

Often in the past and sometimes recent also, the energy has been diluted by negativity and, therefore, turned into a dense mass of consciousness as opposed to a light mass. Conflict through the ages has been a belief system that was built up gradually as people had a more aggressive tribal nature, based on their need of survival. This tribal nature led to conflict as a more predominate energy force. It influenced people's ways of believing what life was and should be, so they never realized that there were more peaceful alternatives.

Some could argue that conflict is still endemic in life and that nothing much has changed. I would certainly agree to a point; however, though there may still be conflict here, many people are of the belief that conflict does not have to be a part of life and rather than live through survival, they choose to live life. This has changed the energy into something lighter and has and continues to change how the dynamics of creation are working out for you all.

This All Began Based on What You Believed in, and It Is What You Feel You Deserve.

Whilst you were in spirit and you were gathering all the information that has inexorably become the life that you are living, you looked at all the emotional formulas that would match up with the life experiences that you were going to have, and with these emotions you deemed what you were worthy of for that life. Everything that has so far transpired in your life was based on your plan and what you felt you deserved.

So, Tabaash, what are you saying here? That I believe that I deserved pain and suffering, illness and poverty, rape, torture and abusive parents, corrupt governments and nuclear weapons of mass destruction, inflation, economic recession, obesity and ignorance, murder, blindness, bad skin, and self-doubt, self-destruction?

It is not so much that you deserve it, but more that you have chosen the path of your life, and you did this because it gave you experiences to learn and to evolve. It is never a punishment but always a choice that enables you to experience all of your selves on the many and varied levels.

The supposed bad things that happen to people are not bad things. They are events that occur through choice, based on what you believe you need to learn, and you are not being punished.

Once you switch all the lights on, you can see much better. When you see better, you are in a position where you are able to make better choices. If you are making choices when you are stumbling around in the darkness, then it's all going to be rather a cacophony of maybe rather than a plethora of certainty. Your base plan for life is that "you deserve." As you evolve this plan, you are able to change your life because you believe differently, which consequently changes the direction of your life.

Everything You Have So Far Undertaken in Life Is an Achievement.

As you progress in your life, you will re-evaluate your perspective on what you deserve, and you will attract to you other aspects of self that will assist you in this process. Since everything is energy that is there for the purpose of creating, you are able to create an aspect of self if you find the need to do so. It is a great thing that source energy is malleable, making it possible for it to become anything that you so desire.

Here are some pointers you may wish to consider that may assist you in the process of change:

- How have I changed, and because of the changes what new ways of thinking do I need to establish?

- What new ways do I need to embrace to be a creator and participator in life?

- Now that I have harmony, what do I see I deserve?

- How does believing differently change the way I see people?

- I know that I deserve all that is good, so what is the best way at this point in my life to enable me to have all this?

An essential point to make here is that having created, you can change it. You have many futures to access in your life, and your creations will define which of those futures you are accessing. You should never feel that simply because you have made a choice, you will vanquish all other choices. As I have mentioned previously, all of everything is always with you. Don't be locked into a pattern that has served its purpose. Always be on the look-out for all those choices!

This Place You Are in Is a Launching Pad for So Much More.

Being in the present is more vital than you can imagine. The present is a point of consciousness where all dimensions converge, therefore, immersing the soul in its divinity. In fact, this is the most important place you can ever be because all your power is available to you in this place, and in the most unconditional of ways! When you are in alignment, the main switch is on, flooding you with the very source of life that all of your selves know as truth.

The present allows you a platform to the past and future.

The present is the point of consciousness that allows you total access to everything. It's the greatest point of reference that you can have available. Without it, you would be utterly stuck in the past or getting too far ahead of yourself by paying too much attention to the future. Being too wedged into the past distracts you from the power of the present and simply engages your attention with emotions that you have already experienced. This will not profit you at all as it is something that has already been, and you cannot be again what you were. You cannot evolve from this way of being as it keeps you locked into the loop of old energy which has no conscious value to you now.

When your issues are resolved and you have total appreciation of what they meant, you are then placed in creation alignment.

Creation alignment is established when you are present to the positive power of your choices. The energy of creation is attracted to this alignment, and it bombards all the senses with ideas, feelings, encouragement and many other stimulants that assist you in what you are creating or want to create. In a way it is no different than the process of human procreation. Once the seed is sown, an astonishing process of creation begins, and once it is totally established, it manifests life. There is a total alignment going on with the physiological make-up of the mother and the soul of the child. There is an agreement of creation between the two sources and even greater agreement between the mother, the soul of the baby and GOD. In the case of your creating, God is the parent and you the soul, merging and creating an ultimate energy that brings about more life in ways more harmoniously.

It is the power of God that makes life manifest on all levels.

It is the power of God that often can make a woman feel quite elated through pregnancy as she is making many non-physical connections during this time in her life. In fact, this state of elation can be experienced through artistic, academic and athletic accomplishments as well. As creators, it is what you are programmed to experience.

This Is All Your Own Choice.

All the choices in your life that have become your expression carry a very unique frequency that is relevant to the way you wish to evolve from that particular point of choice. Take, for instance, that now as you read this book, there is already an established energy that you are partaking. This has placed certain aspects of you into differing states of consciousness. The part that is ready is the conscious part of you. As you pause for a moment to ponder a point or to form a question, you are engaging in an aspect of self that holds an energy that relates to thinking and questioning. You utilize the aspects of your consciousness that are needed for the experience that you are having.

All around you are fields of energy doing a merry dance as they are positioned, based on the need. The way you are attending to the book, the environment you are in, the chair you are sitting in, what you are wearing and more make up the energies that become your "reading experience." This holds you in a pattern of energy that defines the experience that you will have. All the ways you arrange your life and its experiences will influence that very experience. You are always adjusting the energy as the climate of the experience alters. You may close a window because it is too drafty or turn some gentle music on or make a hot drink. All of this is adding and altering the energy of what you are participating in.

Life is full of distractions, but even those distractions are created by you.

Distractions are the human nature's way of keeping you attached to the vibrations that take you away from the God energy. They are the things that you create because of the many and varied excuses you have fashioned to put off the moment that you take complete responsibility for your choices. Of course, distraction has its own personal energy as well, and the more you allow yourself to be distracted, the more you will create a great relationship with it. And then it simply moves in rent-free and becomes a part of your life. The more you are distracted, the less likely you are to concentrate on the things that you really want to achieve, and you end up with lots of loose ends, incomplete projects, ideas that never amount to anything, etc. The list can go on. You may ask what sort of power does human nature have that this happens? In short, it has none at all; it is simply a choice you have made, therefore, building that energy into your belief system.

So one seems to be involved in this rather astonishing dance of energy that is both complex as it is simple. And all of it is founded on the fact that it is all your own choice, created from the energy of free will that comes from the omnipotent supremacy that is God.

CHAPTER SIX

It seems like everyone is swimming in high vibration frequencies!

Tabaash

In 1973 when I was thirteen years old, my parents separated and changed our lives forever. In regards to this, I have often thought about the fact that as spirit we make all plans for our lives choosing the issues and how they will influence us. So what was it about my soul that wanted my father to step out of my life? From the moment they separated though, he ceased to have any major influence in my life, and I was left floundering on my own—not a good thing when you are thirteen, afraid, and stepping into more of an adult world. I don't recall feeling majorly upset about it, which might seem odd. I simply accepted the fact and adjusted to his not being there, but I'm pretty sure that it had a huge effect on me on more subtle levels that affected me as I grew up.

As an adult, I look back and feel rather robbed now of his presence in my life. There was no male mentor in my life—no one that I could look up to and talk to, no one that could help me make that all important transition from boy to man. Fathers are there to teach boys how to be men, and mothers to teach girls how to be women. Neither is properly qualified to do the job of the other, regardless of how many parental skills they may have. I see now that I was rather thrown out to sea and told to swim. It never occurred to me how my siblings were feeling; I took it for granted that we all dealt with it in the same way. I suppose the experience matured me and made me closer to my own source. It made me more conscious of the fact that we all stand alone. It also taught me to be a greater observer of people. My parents never once asked me how I felt. I am not sure if they knew how we were coping as kids.

My mother got a job and worked through the day. We became latchkey kids and had a weekend father. When I was fifteen, we moved from our first New Zealand house. Life became survival, high school, dreams and plans and wanting to get on with something that I had a feeling about but no idea what it was. Wanting to get away from the way that life had become. I was feeling blank and lost and unsettled. I was not happy and stood very alone in my life. At that point in my life, I had no conscious awareness of spirit. I still believed in God but no longer attended church. I gave up Sea Scouts and seemed to be paddling around and around, trying hard to find something to hold onto, but there was never anything to grasp.

I so wanted to be with my father, but that seemed an impossibility. I felt thoroughly swamped by my mother's attention to drama and her insecurities and pressured by her reliance on me. I was trying to grow up but felt like I was raising my mother. Then she really threw us into the lion's den by making a choice that was to alter everything for the worse and challenge me in ways that I never thought would be possible.

Ever on the lookout for love and security, my mother had been corresponding with a man from Wellington, the capitol city of New Zealand. They had been communicating for only a matter of months, and inevitably he came up to Auckland to meet my mother and within hours of that meeting, they were engaged to be married, and we were to all move down the island to Wellington. So once more, we as children had to follow someone else's needs and dreams, leave our schools, our friends, our routines and, in this case, our father.

The memory of saying goodbye to my father on a hot Auckland day a week before Christmas is etched in my mind. I did not cry, but he did—great rolling tears, rolling down his beautiful face. It was the only time I had ever seen him cry, and it gripped me like a vice squeezing the breath from me. My sister and I exchanged glances and held him hard but at the same time wanted to respect the grief that he was obviously feeling. Now I wish I had said more. I wish I had held him longer. I wished more than anything that I could have stayed and lived with him instead of being guided my mother's needs and insecurities.

The trip down to Wellington I remember specifically for two things. It was only a few days before Christmas, and that I had bronchitis. My poor heart chakra was obviously broken and screaming at me, full of emotional congestion and grief. It was mirroring exactly what I was feeling—interesting to note that in those first months in Wellington, I had bronchitis a lot. As it turned out, we went to the home of an alcoholic bully widower with two teenage children. It wasn't long before my mother sent my sister back to Auckland to live with my father as she was developing fast under the influence of my mother's fiancé's daughter. My brothers were young enough to be liked by my mother's husband-to-be. Me? Well, let's just say he didn't take to me and to quote what he said to me once, "Your la-de-da sophisticated ways." My sister was set up nicely, and my brothers were fine. I had nowhere to escape.

One time he had been drinking a lot, and there were people over to watch some of his home movies as he was an amateur photographer and to give him credit that he had a talent. A girlfriend of mine had come over, and we were laughing and watching all the funny antics in the movies, etc.

After my girlfriend left, he really laid into me, accusing me of laughing at him and making him look like a fool. Then he started telling me that I thought I was so much better than anybody else and that I looked down on him and didn't respect him at all. I was completely floored and speechless as I genuinely thought we were all having a good time, and everyone was getting into the swing of things. Everybody there had been laughing along as well. How wrong could I have been?

There was no point in arguing my case or defending myself against his anger at me, so I just walked out and walked down the street, leaving all that vitriol behind me. It was quite late, and there was no one around.

I walked to the end of the road and sat down on a low stonewall and thought. "What I had been thrown into here? If this was the way of things, then what sort of future did I have with this man, and if my mother actually married him, what sort of future did she have? How could she have been so naïve and presumptuous that after such a short courtship, there was some big happy ending?"

I sat there for some time, feeling really defeated and suspended. I felt blank and lost and shocked at what was happening. What was I supposed to do, where else could I go? I lit a cigarette and watched the smoke in the still night air. A police car drove slowly by and stopped as they saw me, sitting there alone in the middle of the night. I must have looked very miserable as one officer in a concerned voice asked me if I was okay. Very good question I asked myself.

To him I said, "Yeah, I'm fine and then stood up and walked back to the house."

I have laughed in the past about what would have transpired had I brought the police back to the house and situation. At the time though it was hardly a laughing matter. There was never any physical violence; it was just all the mental and verbal abuse that was there like a heavy fog, making everything seem rather damp and lifeless. The man obviously had issues that he had never dealt with, and perhaps he himself was thinking he was rather premature in his assumptions about life with my mother.

He evidently assumed that my mother would step into the role as homemaker and mother to his teenage children and dutiful wife to him; whereas, my mother was needing someone to look after her and her children and give her the love and security that she so wanted. This whole debacle carried on for a few more months until eventually my mother came to her senses and broke off the engagement, and so once again we were on the move.

I had two jobs that summer. I would get up early and walk to the local supermarket in Lower Hutt and clean and polish the floors before it opened up for business. Later in the afternoon, I would take the train into the city and clean fourteen floors of toilets, men's side and then ladies. I think it must have been some sort of weird apprenticeship for me. I was cleaning up other peoples crap then, and in a way I suppose I still am!

For a while I also worked in the supermarket after school at the checkout loading up the groceries, I soon discovered that I was being underpaid so I mentioned this to the manager who was very dismissive and brushed me off.

I thought right away, "You little twerp. I'll show you."

So what did I do? I wrote a letter to the Prime Minister, and to my utter surprise he actually wrote back to me personally saying he would look into the matter. And you know, he did! Bless you, Rob Muldoon. I wish I could have been in the manager's office when he opened the letter from the PM. After that I received the proper wage and back pay as well. The manager left me alone after that though he looked at me strangely and with hostility, as did other members of the staff. All those jobs were too much after a while, and so I gave up the supermarket and felt much better cleaning toilets!

What I did was unusual in those days in New Zealand. Someone my age would have kept his mouth shut and put up with it. They probably saw me as some sort of troublemaker, stirring things up and not knowing my place in the pecking order. It got my shackles up, as I hated injustice and unfairness. As time went on, I gave up toilets and continued to mop floors, which I did until I left high school.

All those jobs made me more independent and helped me understand that we are all equal, and we all just have to do what we have to do. Hard work I never shied away from. I met some awesome people in my co-workers and held them all in high respect.

It was important for me to have my own money and to be able to create my own routines and structures. For my morning job I would have to get up really early in the morning to walk to the supermarket, and during the winter this meant walking through thick fog or pouring rain. It was during those early morning constitutions that I was once more aware of that "something more" and felt the peace and comfort of spirit as I walked alone on those cold crisp mornings. Spirit was defiantly walking with me and, I felt, protecting me. I could feel the touch of God in a way I had never felt. The God in me was waking up again and wanted to be fed.

Before the God in me could be really wide awake, there were still plenty of human experiences that were needed to form my character and the way that I saw the world. After my mother broke off her relationship, we had to move to an old house in Lower Hutt. We had the barest of essentials—no furniture apart from the beds we slept in, and the place was old and run-down and dark, the garden had an overgrown jungle—it was quite simply awful. Writing this makes me think of the phrase "In order to be something, you have to know what it is to be nothing."

Well, we couldn't get any more "nothing" than what we were experiencing at that time. It was a nothing house and a nothing feeling and a real nothing time in my life—not wanting to ever be a victim, I got on with things the best I could. I went to school, had my job, and when at "home" stayed in my room all the time, as there was nothing much we could do. We had a radio but no television. I painted my room black and silver with some paint I had found in an old shed at the back of the jungle garden. I filled my walls with posters of rock bands and Farah Fawcett! I read a great deal and kept to myself.

I felt ashamed and despondent by this poverty that had embraced us. Never would I invite anyone over—that not being difficult as my friends were few. I went nowhere and kept to myself. God, where do you go from this place? I was proud and stubborn, and the whole nothingness of the situation overwhelmed me. My mother worked and when she came home was exhausted. I did all the cooking. My brothers were growing up without any good adult male influence and were running riot. There no longer was any family unit, and to me it didn't even feel like a family anymore. We were all broken up and scattered into so many pieces that would never come back together again. It was a sad state of affairs, but there it was. It couldn't get any more black and white than that.

Often when I am at airports, I will look at the people around me and wonder what their story is that has taken them to the point of the life they are in. What were their backgrounds like? What things did they have to grow up with that established their attitudes, fears, ideas and doubts? How many of them had really moved on, and how many were still victims of their pasts? Being a victim of what was seems to be quite an addiction for some people. One can see that there are a great deal of people dragging the barges of the past with them, and the influences of these barges keeps them locked into an energy that makes them servants to the old energy.

Yet we all have within us this something more I have spoken of that impels us to evolve and improve, despite what we have gone through. Some may call it "the survival instinct," that is, a very human-nature-based way of looking at things. I know it's the God nature in us all, telling us to make changes and impelling us to make changes in our lives that move us away from those old attitudes. This higher nature in us all is natural; it's what we all are and we do know this. That's why we find ways of pulling ourselves up from places we never thought we could survive. And of those who don't survive and those who prefer to live out their lives as victims, well, as Tabaash would say. "They are just gods doing it that way."

A few years ago, I was a volunteer at our local hospice. I recall waking up one morning literally feeling that I HAD to do this. Up to that point I had never considered such an idea, and so I rang up a friend I knew was a volunteer, and she gave me the number to ring. I made the call and was put through to the volunteers' manager. I must have talked to this woman for about two hours.

Through the conversation she kept saying, "I never talk to prospective volunteers for so long. I usually get the details and send them the form to fill out."

She dispensed with the idea of sending the form and instead made an appointment for me to see her the next day. Up I went and a few hours later she accepted me as a volunteer.

I loved it. I had no idea what was expected of me, but I did many things. I fed patients, answered the phone, made beds, cleaned and talked, did the dishes. All those years of being a teenage domestic God were coming in handy!

And I thank myself for all the years of reading women's magazines whilst at the gym on the cardio machines. It gave me enough gossip fodder so I could prattle away with some of the older women patients at hospice. A whole ward would dish the dirt on the latest naughty celeb, what was up with the soaps, and who was sleeping with whom. It was a blast!

Death is such a great leveller. I recall one patient who was there for about a month whom I got to know really well. We became good friends in the last month of her life. My shift was Friday night 5-9pm, and when I was finished, I would always go and say goodnight to Hazel.

She would without fail always say, "Well I won't be here next week, so we better say goodbye now," and then roll her eyes heavenward and laugh with a sigh.

One night she said to me, "Blair, isn't it strange that at this point in my life when I am dying that we have become friends?"

I thought for a moment and then replied, "Well, I think that as people, we always attract to us those we need and when we need them, so we obviously needed to know each other at this point in our lives.

And we do, don't we? That's why I can't believe that there are any wrong people in our lives. We attract to ourselves exactly those we need, whether we like them or not! I felt very privileged to be there amongst those people at a time that they were saying farewell to their own lives. The energy of death was so intimate, and I felt that I had transcended time while I was amongst it. I could feel the door to that "something more" was wide open all the time, and it filled me with a sense of awe and, of course, greater curiosity.

I was honoured to be with one lady when she actually died. I had brought her a cup of tea; she was sitting up in bed looking very elegant and very much alive. As I placed the tea on the bedside table, we chatted and then she asked if I could adjust the blinds as the sun was shining in her face. I turned for the briefest moment to do so and in that time, she died. I turned around, and she was sitting up in bed, leaning against the pillows, her eyes a wide stare.

For a moment I was stunned and then said, "What about your tea?!"

Afterwards when I was packing up her belongings, I thought, "All these things that I'm packing now belong to your past, and they are just things now, not personal effects."

In a moment the woman that she was and all the life that she had lived was no more. All those things I packed into a small paper bag, and I could not help but think "Your life for this moment has become this paper bag. You are spirit now, and everything that your life had been is now complete."

I then recalled reading about how people choose who is around when they die. So why did she choose me? Had we some sort of past life connection, was it my energy, did she somehow sense on some level that I knew about the "something more"? I stayed on as a volunteer for a year, and then the feeling came to me that it was time to leave and so I resigned.

Some years later when I was an established channel, I facilitated a workshop with two doctors on Death and Dying and Grief and Loss called "Traveling Light." I was so glad of the time that I had at the hospice as this gave me empathy and understanding of the situation. Spirit had guided me there, preparing me for different roles I would play in my life as a channel.

I also had a job for a while at Wellington Hospital as a theatre aide. The basics of the job were cleaning up after the operations and hanging around in case you were needed for something. So, I had gone from cleaning up people's crap to cleaning up their discarded innards! I have wondered what I had done in some of my past lives to create such situations!

I found it all incredibly interesting watching the operations, getting the feeling of people's souls whilst they were under anaesthesia. One week while I was on night duty, it was quiet and nothing much was happening. I took to wandering around the vacant theatres, cleansing them of the old energies I could feel had been left behind. In particular I felt this energy the most where brain and heart operations had been carried out. When a patient died during the operation, I always made sure I blessed the theatre and cleared the energy. One patient who died was still in the room while I was cleaning up, as the people from the morgue had not yet collected the body. As I was cleaning up, the body would occasionally let out a sigh or a moan as all the gases and air settled down!

Later on a nurse gave me his glasses and pajamas to take back to the ward. Yet another paper bag, another chain of events set up by this person's choice to go home to spirit.

Imagine for a moment that everyone on this planet is floating on a tempestuous ocean in a great storm of energy, and all and sundry are looking for the best way to ride out this storm. All will experience this turbulence based on the formula of life they are presently in agreement with. Each formula is engaged in smaller formulas that draw from ideas and past emotional experiences on all levels. The formula is unique to each person, and so the reality of how that individual rides the storm and the outcome of that ride/trip will be defined by what the person creates.

What is presently occurring on Earth now has never happened before. As has been stated previously, all was one point of consciousness that gave everyone and everything access to the collective vibration of God that is prevalent through life on Earth. In the energy is the power to create and the power to know and the power to exist without conditions that engender limitations. The process of creating life on Earth has been a gradual one over time, and the responsibility of twelve groups of souls that I will call "families."

First Family were the very first wave of souls to experience life on Earth, and they possessed the undiluted energy of God. These souls had creation experience on other planets and in other dimensions and so deemed to be suitable candidates for the creation of life on Earth. They were presented with a basic formula, and as one can see through history, they were very experimental! As they were creating, they had to take into account the compatibility of all life forms. After all, one cannot just throw any life form together and assume that it will be compatible. One would also have to create life that is complementary to the atmosphere and the vibration of Earth. In the earliest stages of creation, the vibration was higher and finer, and so life forms were created to suit that. It was a bit of trial and error, but eventually a formula was found that was suitable and allowed evolution. As the planet developed and evolved, other waves of souls came to Earth.

Let's call these Second Family, Third Family, etc. As each soul family came, they brought a specific energy that enhanced the energy of Earth and the life forms that were being established. The energy was always positive and always connected to the god source. All was harmonious, and life had a rhythm on Earth that sang.

And Then It All Began To Change

Earth was a ubiquitous jewel in the universe, a place of such beauty and grandeur and a place where souls could find uniqueness in physical expression. Those of First Family felt a special connection to the energy as they experienced Earth in its most pristine of states, and some of those First Family souls are alive now. They feel a special attachment and are often involved in careers that reflect their love of nature, humanity and the naturalness of all. They hold Earth in their soul in a true and authentic way, as they knew Earth in its very beginnings.

After the first twelve levels of souls came, others that followed began to be too involved in the physical life on Earth, and they placed more importance on that rather than the harmony of God through the physical. This began to lead to a form of dilution of God's power that at that time flowed through the bodies, and the people began to move further away from the light. The more you move away from the light the harder, it is to see where you stand and where you are going.

To begin with, these souls lived from the point of light, and they carried consciously all the information of life. As the energy became diluted, this one point of light created a point of separation. Place in your mind the idea of concentric circles moving away from you. As each circle expands, it creates a gap between the others. This is what happened on Earth. People became so involved in the human nature that they dispersed the god nature into many dimensions that were beyond their conscious reach. The consequence of this is that they no longer had easy access to the God nature and the information of life that had been available to them naturally.

Access to some of the dimensions was still attainable due to the fact that there was what I shall call *energy bridges.* Theses bridges were, in fact, people who still had the original link to the God source. They were able to access information from source, so as to guide and direct those people who had moved away from the light. The unfortunate thing about this was that people of the time relied too heavily on these souls, and so the pressure was enormous. These souls began to withdraw from the energies of those who were denser, and they formed communities of like-minded beings who still resonated to the original frequency. These communities were established in secret locations so as to protect themselves and the information that they held. As humanity became denser in its energy, the original information that all came with, began to be seen as legend or folklore. After religions were created by people, then the original information was seen as evil and heresy. On occasions one of the light beings as we shall call them, would emerge into the world in an attempt to once again raise the level of light to its original form. The effect of this was that they were often persecuted by religious leaders of the day, and the information that was being taught was seen as dangerous and subversive. They were also often revered as great and God-like and seen by the masses as something that was beyond them as opposed to a reminder of what all beings actually were in their authentic state.

And so Earth and its people were plunged into a time of darkness and density. Destruction, conflict, ignorance and fear became the energies that people embraced, and belief systems were created from this way of living. Control of their lives was often given over to those who through their own egos embraced the veneration that was heaped upon them. The result of all this was that the source energy became more and more difficult to access. Thus, there was further separation from source power, making it more complex for people to have contact with what became known as *higher truth, higher knowledge,* and, of course, *divine wisdom.*

Conflict became rife around the planet, and throughout history has had a devastating effect not just on the people of Earth but in and on the very Earth itself. The death toll from World War One was more than 16 million people with some deaths indirectly caused by starvation, disease and crime. The toll from World War Two has been suggested in the vicinity of 56 million. The toll for the Korean War from both military and civilian deaths was more than 10 million. This, of course, is not taking into account all the wars through ancient and modern history, and they are still being played out. The numbers are speculative, and the actual total would probably exceed what is suggested. It's not just the death, of course, it's the upheaval that all of this causes. The devastation on people's lives, the effect it all has on the land, the eco-systems, and the emotional toll it takes on many, too many generations. And yet the fight keeps going on as new generations are taught to hate, take revenge and keep the fight going. It's what happens when you turn all the lights off.

And so the energy gets denser, and it gets darker, and the people can no longer see anymore or trust anymore. They don't know what to believe, what or whom to trust, and so everything is plunged yet into more despair and more tragedy. And this all happened because people pulled away from the source of life. Over the last fifty years, there has been a positive development in turning the lights back on! Once again there is an awakening to the God energy, and so the process of separation is now reversing.

How has this awakening come about?

It's all in the formula actually. You get enough vibrations working together that are of a higher frequency, and this energy begins to influence the collective consciousness in a beneficial way. As souls are reborn with more enlightenment, they bring with them this new energy that redefines what was and establishes an energy that is a powerful launching pad for something better. These souls bring with them knowledge and awareness that brings people back to the source light.

As the God in you grows it changes the way that you perceive your human nature.

So human nature is being perceived differently because the influence of higher energy is more prevalent. It's no easy ride though, as so many are discovering. Even the best of your abilities and intentions are time and time again being tested as this enormous wake-up call tolls, and people sit up and take notice of what is happening and of what has to happen. All the indicators are now there that are bringing to your attention that there has to be a drastic change in the way that people are thinking, feeling and living, a change that brings about a whole new model of reality. As I said, it is like a giant storm in process, and all are having to find the best way that they can ride it out. As they do, all the cards are being laid out. People are riding this storm in diverse ways but whatever their way, it is still a method that the soul has chosen based on its own believe systems.

The Storm Riders

The Cruise Ship

For those who are on a cruise ship, they hardly notice that there is any storm at all. They are in a place where there is a perfect balance, so nothing will upset what they have created. There are different sorts of passengers on this cruise ship though. They all perceive where they are in many diverse ways, and their actions towards others tell a great deal about who they are.

There are passengers on this ship that are totally in harmony with who they are as God. These souls have their lives balanced, and they are aware that they have created this perfect reality for themselves, and they know that this is OK and simply part of the natural state of things. Life is there for them, and they enjoy the comfort and the harmony that they have created. They take nothing for granted though, and they are aware that if they do for a moment, then they will have a very different ride on the ship. They are also conscious that in their position they can serve others, and so they will seek ways of being philanthropic. The ship offers them opportunities on all levels to learn, observe and serve in the highest possible way. By creating what they have, they are able to access a different view of life and, therefore, offer others who are not so fortunate the chance to change their reality, and if not change it, then to assist them in ways of making those less fortunate have easier journeys. They are able to observe what is going on for other people and the way that they are choosing to ride out the storm. They are aware that there is a storm, and there are those who may be in danger. They are conscious that in some cases they are unable to help, but they know that they are able to throw out a lifeline that can help others through the worst of the storm. They will carry when they can, give life when needed, and assist in any way that they know is plausible and natural. They will never march into anyone's territory without permission. They go full steam ahead in the life that they are living, knowing that they have a responsibility to literally and always "be their brother's keeper."

Then there are those on the liner that simply cannot believe their luck. Here they find themselves with everything at their disposal, and they just lap it up! They have all the comfort they need, plenty of food and security. As long as they are all right, that's fine. They enjoy everything that's on-board and occasionally moan when dinner's not on time or the maid's late for the laundry. They spend plenty at all the shops on the ship; they go to all of the shows and participate in all the ship has to offer. They are unaware that there is a storm going on—for them, it's all about "ME." They do have a sense that other people are out there, but they are so self-absorbed that they give them no consideration at all. They get angry because the pool has been closed due to inclement weather. They are annoyed when the sun does not shine, and they can't lounge around "relaxing." If they do happen to notice there is a storm and other people are involved, their attitude is "At least it's not happening to me."

If something happens to upset their journey and their personal comfort, they will be the first in line to complain, want their money back, and sue the company as well. And for the rest of their lives, they will moan and groan about it and make sure that everybody knows!

And then there are those on the cruise ship who always feel terribly guilty that they are there at all. They are aware that there is a storm, and they feel that they should "sacrifice" their place on board for those who are less fortunate or who "deserve" it more than they do. They keep looking over the side of the liner to see who may need help, and they often get taken advantage of by others, usually be the ones who believe they deserve everything, and it's their right to have it! If there is ever a shortage of anything, they are the first ones to give up something to make someone else happy. They actually know and like that fact that they are on the ship but just can't get away from the feeling and idea that there are others who are more deserving and so even though they are able to ride out the storm in relative comfort, they have created an inner storm that gives them internal soul sickness.

The Pleasure Craft

The people who are on the pleasure craft know that there is a storm, and they do feel it. The ship is big enough to ride the storm but small enough to feel when the waves hit. For those on board this ship, it's about hands on the wheel and keeping things aligned so that they don't get too tossed around. There is still a great deal of comfort on this ship, but on occasions the people have to don wet weather gear as everyone has to pull their weight to keep things afloat. These people take nothing for granted and are very conscious that there are those who are worse off.

They will survive the storm, but they know that times are changing. They see all around them others who are in need of help, so they do what they can when they can.

The Row Boat

Well? It's better than nothing? That could be the sentiments of those who find themselves rowing through the storm. If you are there, you have your work cut out for you as you have to be very strong to keep rowing this boat. You are often pummelled by the waves and blown off course more times than you want to recall.

You are totally exposed to the elements and at times you simply want to give up, for it seems too much of a struggle. At times those from the pleasure craft may render assistance, so do keep an eye out for them. It's hard to see and get a sense of your bearings when you are rowing through a storm. Sometimes you feel you are just rowing and getting nowhere at all and have no idea of any direction. As long as you can get a focal point, you have something to row towards and for. You have to be careful about the cruise liner though as it can't see you, and since it's ploughing through the storm, you might get upended in its wake. If you are rowing, then keep your wits about you. You must always need a plan and really must pay daily heed to this plan.

Some in these rowboats may be upended at times, and the boat may be smashed by the waves. It does not mean the end is at hand though as these people tend to be excellent swimmers, and they have everything in them that enables them to swim through the storm. Though battered and bruised, they will come out of it a winner and move on to do great things.

In the Water with Something to Hold Onto

These souls are barely holding on, but at least they do have something to hold onto! They are being tossed all over the place by what's going on, and when great waves crash upon them, they dive for cover and then resurface, wetter, more tired but still holding on. They may have lost a great deal in their lives, and they even may have very little to show for their lives, but they do have something to hold onto, so that it enables to always find a place where they can hold on and build again. It's wet, and it's miserable and on occasions a rowboat may come their way and pick them up if there is room. These souls have a life buoy in them that they cling onto, and they live in the hope that it will give them new life.

In the Water and Can Swim

As long as you can swim, you still have a good chance of getting somewhere. Some of the waves are really big though, and you have to be a master at holding your breath as the waves strike you. Some have mastered the art of swimming under the wave as it approaches. You may also learn to ride the wave. You may feel at times resigned to your fate, but you never let go of the thread of possibility that there is still a lot possible for you.

In the Water and Can't Swim

These souls seem to have lost all hope of ever surviving the storm. They can't swim and unless others rescue them, then the journey will end for them. The storm is too big for them, and they don't have the energy or the resources to survive. For those around who are in better positions, it's important to keep an eye out for those who can't swim. Although you are not responsible for them, it is a life duty to help in the ways that you can. For those that can't swim, it is your duty to be aware that there are those that can help and will help, and it's important that you never give up. There are always lifelines available to you.

It's hard though at times to be aware of these life lines as you feel so exhausted by the whole process that you are going through. You may not see the point as the waves get bigger and toss you around. They seem to take you further away from what you want and how you want life to be. If you are ever in this place, it's vital to never give up. As you extend energy out of life, you attract people to you that are good swimming teachers. This is a good start to create choices where you feel you have none. You may place yourself in the hands of others for a while until you learn to swim. There will be those, however, that will give up and go home to God.

When the Storm Is Over

When a storm is over, there is always a very odd sort of calm that pervades the environment, its surroundings and the people. Everyone and everything has been tossed and churned for such a long time, and then unexpectedly the storm abates and stillness prevails. For those who have survived the storm, it dawns on them that they have and they begin to look around. They become aware of other survivors and the state of life and everyone around them. Having gotten their bearings once again, they make for land. Once on shore they realize they have to establish the new position. Questions run through their minds:

- Where am I now in life?
- What's the next step for me?
- What is left that I can work with?
- What is the new rhythm?

All survivors will look for each other. It's a magnetism, pulling them all together to establish safety and companionship: a collective energy of hope and relief prevails. Whilst the storm was raging, all needed to pay attention to themselves and how to survive. Now the collective energy creates the need to help each other, and so all reach out and feel the bond that has been established. A soul connection has been made, and there is a great sense of familiarity as all have been in the same storm and survived.

CHAPTER SEVEN

If you're going to have the knowing, don't forget to do the growing.

Tabaash

We stayed in that grotty old house in Lower Hutt for almost a year, and then we moved up on the hill to a better place. It was overlooking the river surrounded by bush, and you could see the hills from all the front windows. The inside was all panelled in oak and had a very nice "Old English" feel to it. The rooms were large and airy, and it had a nice "home" feeling about it. We seemed to be moving away from that awful time, and I felt more settled than I had been for some years. It had a great kitchen, and I did most of the cooking and enjoyed creating concoctions and trying them out on the family. I was sixteen going on seventeen and in the year that I crammed in so much living and learning. As I write this, I am amazed at myself and what I had achieved under so many difficulties.

I went out with a woman from the meat department of the supermarket, but that didn't last too long. I went to a summer drama camp for a week and fell in love for the first time in my life with a woman whom I adored. Love was simply wonderful. "A Star Is Born" with Barbra Streisand had just come out, and there was a bath scene where the room was full of candles, steam and love. We replicated this and simply explored.

She came to stay at our place one weekend, and my mother, being very conservative, would not let me share my room with my girlfriend, and so I had to be content with a sleeping bag in the living room. I waited and waited and waited, and then when

I thought it was all quiet and clear, I crept slowly down the panelled hall to my bedroom. I was hardly breathing and conscious of every creak and noise as I took careful steps to my supposed sexual heaven. I was just at the door when my mother whose room was across the hall from mine, flung open the door and DEMANDED that I return back to the celibacy of the living room. Dejected and no doubt frustrated I returned, knowing that there was no point in pleading my case. Funny though, she didn't seem to mind that we were alone in my bedroom with a locked door during the day. Perhaps her mind could only reach to not permitting nocturnal dalliances?

I became a model for Panache Model agency and actually got quite a lot of work. I got a lead in a commercial about this guy who had left school and was having his wages direct credited into a Post Office savings account. I did pretty well through my teens and twenties and managed to score another lead in a commercial this time for Sanatorium Toasted Muesli. And, of course, there were the live fashion parades! One fashion parade was in an outdoor mall, and I was the only male. There were about six women and our changing room was a small trailer. When I had a change, I had to rush breakneck speed to the trailer where I was stripped by the dresser and would emerge in the next outfit. It was such a blast and afterwards a few glasses of wine and a bit of a party would top of the event.

After a year my girlfriend broke off the relationship, and I was suitably devastated. It was my first broken heart, and so I added relationship heartbreak to my list of experiences. How do you mend a broken heart? You don't. You live through it, and eventually you do live to see another day!

During this time my mother had once again been writing to prospective husbands, and eventually she found a little bald be-speckled man in his fifties who had never been married. He was very quiet and conservative, and he consistently smoked a pipe. I was a witness at the wedding and had my suspicions that she was not in love with the man, but I kept my mouth shut and got on as best as I could with this new addition to her life.

I remember well as we got out of the car to go into the church she said, "Well, here we go" in a way that didn't exactly fill me with confidence for her future.

I also recall that as we were all coming out of the church after the ceremony, a group of youths drove by and "mooned" the wedding party. The irony of this was not lost to me!

As my mother settled into her new married life, I was no longer sure of my position at home. Her husband obviously wanted to be the Lord and Master over his domain and so I felt rather superfluous. I never had any particular disagreements with her husband, but the feeling that I was no longer required felt strong. I was in my last year of high school and was in an "in between place" that made me feel like I was in some sort of holding pattern. Life simply became study, friends and the odd modeling assignment. I spent a little time with my father in Auckland during holidays and was glad to connect with him. At home I made friends with some guys up the road from us, and through one of them, I connected with a girl whom I had known briefly in Auckland in my first year of high school, and I ended up seeing her for a few months. We did the usual hanging out with friends, partying, etc., but we rather ran out of steam and the relationship finished.

I seemed to have reached a point in my life where I had outgrown so much and yet had no idea what I was supposed to grow into. I'm sure we all experience this many times in our lives. Growing up and growing away from what was familiar is rather a rite of passage and, of course, we all deal with it in our own ways. With all the ups and downs over the last few years, I was no doubt more insecure than I was letting on, so it was like driving with the handbrake on at times. I knew I was moving into a new phase of my life but had no idea of the script and/or role I would be playing. I wasn't even sure what roles were available to me.

I think now of what Tabaash teaches: we all have many futures, and they are with us all the time. All the events of our lives, of course, emit an energy that attracts certain futures to us. And then, of course, we have definite plans that we have all made for our lives. Plans that will involve certain changes in our circumstances and bring to us challenges that will make us think and feel in ways we never imagined possible. And, of course, these changes often involve bringing new people into our lives, and sometimes meeting these people can completely change our destiny, or perhaps meeting them actually helps us fulfil our destiny. It was at this time in my life that I met Kay.

How do you write about the most important person in your life and give it the justice it deserves? The world is full of people who are unsung heroes—people who are vital threads that hold everything together and yet too often are not recognized as such. Also, how do you write about such an important part of your life, knowing that it involves the lives of so many people while yet wanting to respect their privacy? I sit here and recall so many events and people and responses by those who knew me a long time ago and those who know me now, and I feel I want to do it all justice but still feel the walls of doubt looming.

My wife Kay is one of those unsung heroes. I thought long and hard about how to write this and then realized thinking long and hard was going to take me nowhere. It has to flow and find its own rhythm, and so I have to write through my feelings, not my head. And in a way that really is a good way to describe our relationship over the last thirty-six years. It has had to flow and find its rhythm as we have grown through our life together.

She lived up the road from where I lived with my family and said the first time she saw me was when I was standing at the end of her driveway talking to some other teens from my high-school. They were all in school uniform and I? I was wearing a sarong and a Balinese shirt that my brother-in-law had given to me. This was probably very unusual attire for an eighteen-year-old in New Zealand in the 70s, but I was not exactly made in the same mold as everyone else!

Kay was forty-two, and I knew some of her family and would visit at times. We became friends and discovered we had a lot in common, dancing being one of the things that we both enjoyed.

There wasn't a lot of nightlife in Wellington in 1978, but there was one club that we had heard about that everyone was going to called Ziggies, and Kay and I decided to check it out. Down a dark alley and up some stairs into the world of muted lighting, disco music and life drag shows as it turned out that Ziggies was a show place for all the local drag queens. We became regulars there and would love going to watch the "girls" perform their routines.

One night when we were there, they were short a lightning person and male chorus dancer for the floorshow, and so after a very quick rehearsal, I filled the spot on stage while Kay manned the lights! I learned to have great respect for those "ladies" of Ziggies with their lavender wigs, long false eyelashes, falsies and sparkly dresses. Those girls really put their hearts and souls into what they were creating, and while they were on the stage, you could see they were living the part they were playing. I never saw them as "men in frocks;" they were just themselves and living their own lives. As an eighteen-year-old going on 30, I took all of this in my stride and simply played the role I was playing then.

It was an immense experience of life, connecting with so many diverse and interesting characters. I think that during that time I really started to learn how to talk to people and, in fact, really *feel* what people's lives were all about. With some of the "girls" you could feel a sense of sadness and desperation, which at the time I did not understand, but years later, I could see how lonely some of them must have been in their lives and can only imagine what sort of extreme lives some of them must have been living. Some were rather tragic figures whom I'm sure were caught up in a world of prostitution and drugs, desperate for kindness and security.

I've since discovered that some of these "girls" lived so-called respectable lives as bankers, accountants and the like. They have wives and children and houses in the suburbs.

We all play so many roles through the lives we live, and all these roles are who we are, and through our lives they are like voices that need to be heard. I feel they are aspects of ourselves that need expression, and I believe that we create more of them as we experience life. When we are born, we come with the cornucopia of knowledge that we have brought from the experiences of our other lifetimes. The life we are living now is certainly the deal that we have structured to vent our "voices." We possess a unique qualities that can never be replicated. And it rather seems to me disrespectful to God when we don't make the best effort to be everything. How many of us are really living our full potential now? Our lives are the performances that we are all starring in, and yet we seem to be bit players in our own show sometimes. I think that those performers at Ziggies really had the balls (no pun intended) to get up there on those stages and through their performances belt out who they were and what they were feeling. I'm sure that some people saw them as sad losers who were sick and deviant, but they were real and raw and brave.

We did go to other clubs that started to pop up over town, but there was nothing quite like the exposed honesty of Ziggies. It had soul as the people who performed there did. We were all involved in make-believe and fed each other's needs to be a part of something more.

My relationship with Kay developed beyond the friendship, and as we blended more into each other's lives, we created adventures that would establish our consistently growing connection and sow the seeds for our future life together. I felt I was getting on with life and growing in the process. My connection with Kay put me more in the adult world, and I was socializing more with people ten and twenty years older than me rather than my own peers. I went to school, did my job, and pretty well kept to myself. My mother's marriage seemed to me fairly stable, and there was no disharmony on the home front. I had no sense of where Kay and I were going with the relationship, the future I did not consider. Exam time was looming, and so like thousands of other students in their final year of high school, I hit the books and looked forward to finishing school, leaving home and getting out into the world. I did not have any particular serious idea about what I wanted to choose as a career. I had toyed with the idea of medicine and oceanography and also had considered applying for the New Zealand Drama School. It was mainly a big blank though. I stayed fairly present in my routines and patterns, thinking that there was going to be plenty of time to plan my strategy and fold away my old life and create something new. I had considered a move back to Auckland as well but wasn't clear. And then all of this was rather fast-tracked when one afternoon after having sat an exam, I returned home to find the contents of my room all packed up and placed in bags on the outside porch.

The locks had been changed and on peering into my bedroom window saw that one of my brothers had moved into my room. I banged on the door, and no one came. They had all gone out. I was angry, I was confused, and I was distressed. And not knowing what to do, I just sat on the floor of the porch and waited for everyone to come home.

When they did, they totally ignored me. I could have been invisible as far as they were concerned. I wracked my brains to find what could possibly have gone wrong; I could not come up with anything. It never entered my mind that it may have had anything to do with my relationship with Kay as I had spoken to my mother about it, and she didn't seem particularly perturbed. I wasn't some delinquent that was disrespectful of the parental home and out all night boozing and taking drugs. If I did go out, I always informed them where I was going and was home at a decent hour.

I ended up spending the night in the porch; morning came and still no reply to my knocks. I went to my morning job and then in desperation up the road to Kay's place where I remember breaking down in tears and feeling utterly helpless. I felt like my mother and her husband had thrown me onto the rubbish heap.

"Thanks, Blair, you have served your purpose, but we can't deal with you as an adult, so just piss off."

Thank God I didn't have an exam that day as I was in no fit state for anything. Kay was going away on business, and she arranged for me to stay in a bed and breakfast around the corner from school. It was an old two-story house probably built in the 1900s. It had a turret and though clean and tidy, there I was once again uprooted and seemingly at the mercy of destiny. I distinctly remember the room I was given. It overlooked the street, and there were two single beds. There was no distinctive décor, and the light bulb that hung from the wire in the ceiling was bare. There were plastic flowers in a cheap glass vase, no doubt someone's vain attempt to make the place cheery. You had to share a bathroom. It all seemed to me the sort of place that someone would come to die in.

After a restless night I awoke with bronchitis—my poor heart chakra was screaming with congestion! I wheezed myself through the morning and had to take myself off to school around the corner to sit my final exam. I had to walk a bit and then rest as I could hardly breathe. The school was only five minutes around the corner, but it took me all of half an hour to get there. I sat the exam and left. I said nothing to anybody, and I went back to the death room and slept. I stayed in that place for about four days. I just felt blank. I couldn't stay there all day so had to go out until I was allowed back in. I don't even remember where I went and what I did. I know I never even went to the doctor about the bronchitis. I just put up with it until it cleared.

Kay eventually returned from her business trip, and seeing the state I was in, let me stay for a while with her family. I was in a bad way and had no one to turn to, nowhere to go. I felt desperate and didn't know what to do. I felt weak and powerless, frightened and abandoned, and had no idea at all what lay before me and how I was to cope. It was a very present place but a very heavy place. I wasn't depressed and would never in a billion years ever have considered suicide. That was not my way.

Never had I considered that this would happen to me and particularly in the way that it did. However insecure I may have felt in the odd family arrangement I had lived in, it never entered my mind that I would be thrown out into the cold and told "Go and fend for yourself!" And for it to happen so abruptly. After eighteen years of being with my brothers and my mother, in a moment it was all finished. No goodbyes or good luck. No farewell parties and excited talks about the future and what may lie in front in front of you. The world, of course, is full of young people who have gone through what I went through and some much worse. I'd like to think that most have moved beyond the upheavals and gone out into the world and become successful in life in all the ways that they could.

And there are those, of course, who can't cope and fall into such dense and conflicting patterns that the life they live is nothing but misery and failure. Whatever the case, I still believe that whatever the circumstances, we all have choice and at any time there are always options available to us. It's too easy to get caught up into being a victim of what has happened in life, and, of course, the more we pay attention to what went wrong, the more that energy becomes paramount in our lives. There is no child or teenager or adult who despite the crap that may have been dished out to them can't shift and change and reach out for ways that will help. There is always something or someone to reach out for, and I encourage anyone who finds him or herself in such a position to do so. Your greatest gift is your faith in yourself.

Ask yourself what you believe is the simplest thing you can do right now to make it better. Don't be too urgent about it. Set the pace that you can cope with. Who can be there for you? What can be there for you? Keep it easy, keep it simple, and don't get too far ahead of yourself.

I had Kay to reach out to, and she came to me, seeing I was a person in need. I had so many emotions going on at the time and needed a firm hand to prop me back up. I willingly put myself in her hands and let her do the driving, and she did it well. An organized and efficient woman prone to perfectionism, she took charge of the situation and enabled me to find a platform that I was able to build my life from. However, even though Kay was there, I never talked to anyone about any of what had happened. Social services these days would have had a field day, but then it wasn't like that. You just sort of picked up the pieces and tried your best to put it all back together.

As I'm writing this it occurs to me why did I never contact my father? You know it never even crossed my mind. I think that we were so emotionally distant at that time that the energy between us wasn't there, and he wasn't the person I needed. This had no bearing on the love I had for him, and I'm sure the last thing he wanted in his life was me complicating his world. I'm quite amazed when I look back on my resilience now and what I had to cope with all alone. Sometimes we need to create these sudden shock waves in our lives that propel us into a different future. It absolutely changes the script, and it brings in a whole new host of characters that become a part of your life. Perhaps at times it is the only way that we are able to fulfil what we have come to be and do in this lifetime. As painful and destructive as it seems at the time, it sets up a new road of infinite positive possibilities.

Some therapists would say that I was looking for a parent substitute and the security that I did not have, and to an extent I would have to agree. At that time in my life, I was standing alone in a way I never thought possible, and so it seemed natural to reach for a sense of security that was close at hand. Who amongst us doesn't look for security and comfort in times of distress? Are we not all in some ways wanting to be nurtured, parented, loved and accepted all through our lives, and don't we find this in the people that we create relationships with? We are all fathers and mothers, brothers and sisters to each other, and I believe we bring these roles into all the relationships that we have throughout our lives.

Of course, the karmic implications of all this is interesting. How many times in previous lives have we been our own parents? We continually keep turning the diamond of life, looking to experience yet another facet of the journey of human understanding and experience. And with each relationship, whatever it may be, we all have a chance to discover yet another aspect of who we are as souls. We see for ourselves through the dynamics and diversity of the relationships that we create. I wasn't just looking for someone to look after me; I was involved in a much bigger picture of growth and opportunity to know myself from what I was going through. So I suppose you could say that I was my mother's alcoholic fiancé, and I was the man she eventually married. I was my mother and my father, and so the list goes on.

I was, of course, really looking for who I was and what I was all about, and I was playing all of that out on that emotional battlefield that I had created. This would take me further from my human nature and place my God nature in the forefront. All of us are involved in the same game, but we all have different roles to play so we could bear witness to our own unique evolution. This, of course, leads to accountability and responsibility for the lives that we lead and all that occurs. So if that really is the case, we all must graciously thank ourselves for all the emotional pain, the feelings of despair, the helplessness and the turmoil we have created and realize that all the destruction that we entered into was a part of the lives that we have created.

This is no easy deed to accept when we look at some of what we have created. No one wants to believe that it is our responsibility, and if we continue to see life only through the human nature, then we stay stuck into the patterns that are counter-productive to us. Taking responsibility allows us the stop the pandemonium, and we then can place ourselves in a way where we can get into a better rhythm that will give us the balance to structure and organize our lives better.

I know that in whatever ways, spirit must have been there, guiding and healing me sending me energy that allowed me to cope. I know this to be true. Those nights in the bed and breakfast in that death room when I lay in bed not knowing what was going to happen to me, I felt somehow clear and calm and was still able to be very present and focused. Yes, my life had stopped in some way, but something was saying to me it had begun in another way and that "something" had nothing to do with my human nature.

I feel that my parents failed me in good parenting, but I do see and understand that it was part of the deal that we had all made in this life to allow growth in our lives. I don't blame them in the least, as we all evolved in our own journey and what it entailed. It seems pointless to create the idea of yourself being a victim because of how other people failed in their roles. One has to remember that you put yourself in that position, and everyone was simply playing out the roles that were created. At the end of the day it's best to look at the platform you are standing on and then decide your best course of action through acceptance, positive thinking and action and by participating in a life that encourages you to be a good and successful person, despite what you may have gone through.

And so I began my journey as a rather displaced person. I left school and not being sure of what I was wanting to do, I landed a job in a menswear shop in the city, and after weeks of living with Kay and her family, I moved out and lodged with a family I had known for some years. I stayed in this place until eventually Kay and I moved into a flat together in the city. I used to write a lot of poetry in those days, and I had a desk that had been an old treadle sewing machine. I still had the treadle and as I wrote I found great solace in treading away! I recently came across some of those poems and here is one from 1982.

So cold so dark a dismal day
I walked alone. I walked this way.
The wind so strong, the sea not still,
The houses above, poured from the hill.

No desire had I; my thoughts were few.
From where I stood, I was the old and the new.
Few people about and those that were there
Seemed to sit in their cars
And accusingly stare.

As if to say what right had I
To be alone and walk this way?
To keep myself apart and private?
You have no right to be alone separate and private.

Isn't that simply awful? I was only twenty-two at the time. I recall that day very clearly, walking down to the beach and feeling all that and more. There were quite a few in the same vain, all a bit heart-rending and theatrical. When I read them again, I felt myself blushing with mortification that I could be so melodramatic! However, no doubt I got a lot out of my system writing and treadling away.

TABAASH SPEAKS

Man! Did You Ever Learn to Surf That Wave Fast!

Tabaash

Inevitably all storms come to an end, and when they do, one has to wake up to the fact that everything is going to be different. Sometimes the landscape of life can change so much that one would hardly distinguish anything at all that is familiar, and this can be exceedingly disorientating to begin with. What's very important to acknowledge straight away is that *you have changed*, and there is no going back to how things were before. You are different now, and you have to get used to the notion that you now will see the world in a way unlike any way you have seen before. You are now going to create different realities because the energy is no longer the same, and you won't have the same tools to work with. The canvas of life is also changed so you have new material to work with and on.

Your first task is to be the observer.

Like anyone who wakes up from a tempest, you want to get your bearings as quickly as possible. Then again, you don't want to take the plunge into unchartered territory too quickly, so you must be conscious of observing from a place of peaceful concentration. Observing carefully allows you to get the new picture. As you observe, you are receiving information that you will store up in your brain that gradually starts to paint the new picture. Through your observations, you are piecing together this new landscape that is now your life. The soul self will, of course, hone in on areas that it knows you need to pay special attention to, and so you will find that you will be guided and in this guidance you will establish a magnetism about you that will attract certain situations your way. You begin to recognize after a while the patterns that are emerging, and these new patterns give you more clarity, allowing you to establish new foundations that you will need to build again. Being an observer enables you to assemble new data that is fundamental to any futures that you could create. In your observations there are some significant questions to put to yourself that can assist you on the path that you are forging.

- *What position am I in now?*
- *In what way/ways am I powerful?*
- *What feels most natural for me to do at this point?*
- *What is getting my attention?*

There will be more that you will ask and in your questions and surveillance, I think it is imperative not to place any attention on weakness or conflict. I am a firm believer in paying heed to what is right in your life. Conflict is not a natural idiosyncrasy in human nature on Earth but rather one that was created as people moved further from the source of life.

All through this process you must remember to grieve.

It's essential for any being involved in major change to recognize the emotions that come up and express what they are feeling. To not do so is detrimental to the well-being of your body and your life. Grieving is many things: it's not just the passing of someone. Loss comes in an array of forms and affects people in different ways. Once the storm is over, you will grieve for the loss of what was, knowing that you can never bring life back to the old ways. The old ways are like a dear and loved relation who has passed, and your grief will be genuine. And remember that you are grieving for what *you were*, and you will miss who you were dreadfully at times. And change brings about the need to realize that some things will simply not happen now, and one must grieve for the lost chances and opportunities that are no longer a part of your life.

There is a great deal to mourn at this time in your world. Many people are standing in life where they look around and see that it is all different now. The feeling of how life used to be is no longer there, as all has been so dramatically altered that it's hard to recognize what was once so familiar. People feel the shift of energy so strongly at present, and it's so rapid and so consistent that it's hard to keep up with the changes that are occurring. This puts much pressure on the emotions, and it's very easy for anyone to want to retreat in the face of such challenges and change. As the human body absorbs all of this, it finds its way to release through the emotional state of grief and to do so is like a cleansing of dense energy, allowing the brighter energy of the soul to take precedence.

The human body was not created to sustain hurt in any way. It will find ways to check out if it finds itself under too much pressure.

Some changes can be so swift and sudden that we find ourselves seemingly overnight in a place entirely unlike what was known before. Human nature is interesting in the fact that it has the propensity to adapt quickly; this is the survival tactic found in your soul. One does not need to be in survival mode all the time, and so once that energy is no longer needed, the reality of the changes that have occurred establish themselves in the physical system. There may be an instant result in regards to the expulsion of the old energy, or there may be a delayed reaction that may come about weeks or at times even years after the event. Whatever the case, all emotions have to be expunged from the physical system to ensure well-being.

This is the time to let it all out of your system.

It's clearing the decks really, giving you a nice clean place to create something new without the clutter of a lot of superfluous energy. If you are observing from a place of clutter, it's hard to see through it all, and you end up it pushing aside, and it creates piles on the side that can be precarious as they can fall on you at any moment.

Better to make a complete job of it—delete all old energy out of the system so when you do create, you create from a place of clarity and accord. As an observer of your new circumstances, you give yourself a greater chance and, of course, as your own authentic self, you want to have all the choices possible.

As things start to settle down, you are able to acquire a much better perspective of your situation. The old platform is not only gone but so is much of what you were and how you saw the world, and, of course, how the world saw you. The mirrors have changed, and so you have a whole new set of reflections looking back at you.

You are now seeing yourself in a whole new light.

And this new light is something that one has to accustom oneself to carefully. Too often people will run before they know how to walk. There are many ways that people respond to changes, both positive and negative. Some are productive; others destructive. Imagine it is like meandering through the forest. Your path is wide and clear, and there is nothing that distracts you. Then you come to a part of the path that is obstructed. Now the obstruction could be the most beautiful plant filled with the most intoxicating flowers. Conversely, it may be a giant hedge that is full of thorns and poisons, dense and a dangerous to all who cross its path. With each situation you can approach it in the same way.

You are threatened and challenged, and you want to run from the situation.

Many will do this, afraid of both what is positive for them or destructive. They find the whole situation far too challenging whatever the case may be, and so in desperation they panic and flee, looking for another path to take in the hope it will be less arduous. Many flee from change because they are uncertain about what they are facing and often feel ill-equipped. And the biggest uncertainty is when you face yourself when you are presented with so many new options.

This is why it's so essential that you recognize the need for new belief systems when everything changes. Going for what you have always known does not seem to be advantageous at times, so you must negotiate some new deals with the new selves that have emerged from the changes that have been made. This negotiating enables you to walk carefully towards change with a sense of security with a good core to build afresh.

You plunge in without any consideration for the consequences to you or to anyone else.

It's crucial to consider your options in any case, but regrettably for some this is exactly what they don't do. This leads to yet more dissonance in life, and it becomes more complex in recognizing the best way to use the situation to your advantage. Many simply put up with what is coming their way instead of organizing it to be more beneficial. Making this choice puts you at a disadvantage and will slow the whole process of your journey.

The other drawback to this is that it can often make people stuck in fear and uncertainty. They can become overtly suspicious and worry about the next step just in case it may lead them to more confrontation. This becomes a very crippling experience for some, and so they basically take the plunge because they are afraid that they will be stuck in a place, and taking the plunge is better than nothing at all. People will often take the plunge because they are afraid of where they are, and they think it is the best way to rid themselves of what they don't want to experience anymore. Taking the plunge also puts a great pressure on yourself, and this can have an impact on your mental and physical well-being.

You stand still, observe carefully, and consider your options and what seems most beneficial to you.

This may seem the most obvious of choices, but this does not mean that it's the road that most people will take, particularly when dealing with a sudden shift of consciousness and not being too sure of what the rules are anymore. However, let's imagine that this is the chosen road, and you are now before it. When you stops and observe the new circumstances, you first have to be aware of your own personal responses to the situation. This response is vital to the way you are going to approach things from here on. Having gauged your response and made alterations that are required, you are now in a position to look at what you are working with and what you have made available to yourself in regards to guidance and assistance. For every human being, there will be a plethora of energy available that will come in the guise of people, spirit, books, etc. These will direct you in the ways that can only profit you. I think it's of great consequence to bear in mind that this is a personal experience unique to you from your own platform of creation. And, of course, it is the same for all. There is a definite need to make it personal so that you are able to engage with the energy that will best assist you.

Everything in your life is personal to you. It is impossible for you to be replicated.

The acknowledgment of the personal nature of your experience allows you to have better ownership of your situation. This enhances the way you will direct the course of your life. From a spiritual perspective, it aligns you more fittingly to the form of energy that you may need. This eliminates the need for counter-productive energy links that make take you down a road that is ineffective and unrewarding. When you makes it personal, you really are making it all about you, and this creates a more natural alignment with all you need, so you can often see the results without having to initiate a huge amount of effort. Making it about you engages you with you, the soul, which as you already are aware, has all the answers. You begin to get the desired results without all the toil. This getting personal should be used on a day-to-day basis. To assist you, here are some examples that you might find effective in life's day-to-day events. And remember whatever you affirm, it can only be truly effective to you when you find a way of also *living* your affirmation.

- *Body and Mind, we are no longer involved in that relationship anymore, so we no longer need the old emotional responses.*
- *Body and Mind, we have had the operation now, and so we are well on the road to a full recovery.*

- *Body and Mind, we are moving to a new city, and so we need to let the energy of the old city go and embrace the new one.*

- *Body and Mind, I am moving into a new job and so wish to let you know that you need to adapt to new people and circumstances.*

- *Body and Mind, you are a great magnet for happiness, profit, balance and peace.*

I think you get the picture by now. The body and the mind need to and want to be informed all the time.

What is powerful about you now?

Many people see change as something destructive, something that takes from them the power of choice, the option to make their own decisions. Often when people have changes foisted upon them by circumstances seemingly beyond their control, they become rather defeatist and powerless. They establish a belief that they are weak, and everything has changed for the worst, so what is the point? This is the time when it's essential to affirm what is powerful about your new circumstances and what is your own personal power at this time. The conscious acknowledgment of what is "right in your life" is a good platform to create from. Having established the power of you in the present, you now offer up better views of what your future choices are and what best suits the situations that you are now involved in. You have created a better vantage point from which you are better suited to observe your life.

The majority of people are not paying much conscious attention to themselves and the ways they are powerful in life. Many would feel that by doing so is self-indulgent and ego-based; others would be too embarrassed. Social attitudes frown upon such narcissistic immoderation, so people refrain from paying heed to their personal qualities. Instead, they end up investing in copious amounts of thoughts, words, and deeds that are totally counter-productive. So it seems we have the premise of life being a place of danger, one where we must look out, be on our guard; protect ourselves. Life is out there to get us! Such a platform will only serve to create systems that will limit and degrade you, making you feel that you are always in some sort of combat zone, waiting for the next war to begin. Doing this consistently is going to breed more of the same energy and make life dangerous as the contempt it establishes spreads like a virus amongst others, leading to conflict in the community and, of course, world-wide.

Stop looking at what's wrong and instead look at what's right.

When the systems and structures of life break down, it's because they can no longer be sustained, and it does not mean that they were always wrong. Change comes about because we have outgrown what was and has to be replaced with something new. There's always a point when we have to move on to a more powerful and sustainable way of living in order to gain from the new energy that is being created on this Earth. The recognition of your own authoritative role in this is crucial to the way the new energy settles. All of you should not only be identifying what now makes you more powerful but what also makes everyone and everything powerful. To acknowledge this is recognizing the collectivism that you are participating in. It's this collectivism that unites you all as Gods, placing you all in a position as Gods, the creators whose job is to create the best possible life. And so, from this platform you have situated yourself in such a manner as to feel and see the ease of life and the availability of everything your whole being desires. All is aligned, consequently, making it easy for you to see opportunities and readily embrace the changes, knowing that you will evolve in all the ways you can with the comfort that you know you don't stand alone on this journey. You have the rest of humanity to keep you company.

Today is the best day I have had in my whole life and my whole existence.

The above statement can be deemed as an ultimate way to start the day. What a breakfast to give to your soul! This is exactly the sort of soul nutrition that all of you need to feed yourself. Most people have the tendency to skip this sort of breakfast and just grab any old thing. What your soul really likes is for you to plan a daily menu and to give it the correct nutrition it needs for that day's energy. The menu needs to be varied as your soul does have a rather large appetite, and it gets bored if you keep feeding it the same things time and time again. When you affirm that it is the best day of your life, then you get up into the highest energy that you can have. You have set the standard for the day, and if you affirm this thought through the day (sort of like snacking), your whole being will recognize an appetite for this soul food, and it will let you know what it is partial to.

You will develop a more refined palate and find that your selves will reject anything that is not to their taste. This is not saying that your selves become difficult to please or pernickety but rather they become more aware of what is to their taste. They know that if they feed aptly, they will benefit exceedingly from a diet that gives them dominance over limited energy. A good soul diet consists of everything that makes the Mind, Body and Spirit feast together and, of course, enjoy the company of each other. It's rather like a recipe really. You need all the right ingredients, but you also have to have them portioned properly. If you have too much of one thing and not enough of another, then regardless of the correct recipe, you still end up without the result that you desire. As you grow in life, your appetite for life changes in all ways, and it's vital to recognize when you need to feed the Mind, Body and Spirit differently. Otherwise, you always have a bland diet, and that's not very palatable.

Don't just grab at anything old thing for your soul breakfast.

You give birth to a new self daily, and with this new self you have new chances to live with greater consciousness of your aptitudes. Every soul comes into life with intent, and so the life that you are living is not a boil-in-the-bag experience. Some people are of the understanding that you make it up as you go along, and this is far from the truth. You are all born with your intentions firmly established. Once you have been born, you then institute the best ways that you are able to fulfil those intentions. Every life you have is a planned experience and one that you always want to get the most out of.

Whilst out in spirit, you are quite the strategist, and you deliberate carefully the energies of the new life that you will have. You will always establish the power aspect of life first. These power aspects are the ones that enable you to become successful in the paths that you will choose. It's the positive intent that you would build around the God that you are. This intent is of great consequence to this new life as it creates the base for the magnetism you wish to have through feelings. Everybody is born with astonishing abilities to achieve far more than what most people actually do in their lives. There is no way that the God energy would ever create you as less than what you are, and the God energy would never give you a little bit of life and say, "Well, there you are. Make the most of that and see what happens!"

Once you create the "powerful intention" energy, you are then going to look at what the vocational scheme is going to be in the new life. All souls register their intentions before they are born. They will bring with them the facility to allow them to accomplish the tasks that are positive and powerful; they will conversely bring attachments that may manifest as negative experiences that can have unfavourable effects on their lives. Every day you are faced with what will make you powerful and successful or weak and uninspired—thoughts that could lead you to achieve or fail. You are all involved in this, and there is no exception. To ensure the best deal is struck, it's best that you show real leadership that enables you to manage the day to ensure the best possible outcome.

It is the lack of management that stimulates the negative attachments that you come with, therefore, giving them precedence over anything else. This leads to a weakening of your association with your higher nature, diluting the power of life, and consequently, rendering you confused and uncertain in regards to the best way to run your life. This does not mean that you are in a precarious position, but it unquestionably challenges you, and you find this position puts you in uncertain terms with yourself and all around you. This uncertainty can make people start to reach for stimulants in life that they believe will carry them through the tough times, whereas this choice will often act more to weaken the power and make you more incompetent in managing your life and making positive decisions. People will often grab something to eat on the way to living the day, and you don't want to do the same thing in an emotional and mental level. Your systems crave the suitable nutrition to allow you to be stalwart in creating the most accomplished of days.

Without fail always feed yourselves properly.

CHAPTER EIGHT

How could one possibly consider a conclusion when one is in the midst of life?

Tabaash
___

I began to get bored working at the menswear store and decided that I needed a change that would help me to grow and experience more of the world and people, so I got a job as a waiter in an Italian restaurant called Il Casino. It was owned by a man called Remiro. He was from Venice, ten years older than me, full of life and very worldly. I had never met anyone like him in my life, and he inspired me and motivated me to discover more of myself than I had ever considered before. He also taught me how to smoke and drink and party in ways I did not think possible. He had a huge influence on me, and I grew up more being in his energy .To me, he represented a freedom that I wanted, a new way of being. It was exciting and challenging and liberating. He seemed to know everyone and went everywhere, and his total enthusiasm for life was infectious.

The restaurant sat about eighty people and was on two levels. It was an old narrow building with double hung windows in the front, and fireplaces that roared continually throughout the winter days and evenings. It had charm and glowed with an energy that was right out of Italy. I found I had a forté for the business, and I loved every moment of it: the people the conversations, the atmosphere and the smell of good food cooking. I worked long hours, made good money and had a great time along the way.

I recall the day that Remiro's first son was born. We put up a banner on one of the walls, announcing the birth and then shared a bottle of Moët champagne with Remiro to wet the baby's head. He went back to wife and baby, and the rest of us decided that another bottle of Moët was in order, and then another. There were just three of us working in the afternoon, two in the kitchen and me in front of house. We had anticipated a quiet lunchtime as it was wet and wild outside and usually the lunch trade was quiet on days like that. We were all rather "pissed," to coin a phrase, that to our horror, the restaurant filled to capacity. I really don't know how we did it, but we did. I recall weaving through the restaurant being brilliant and efficient, and highly conversant as I went from table to table in the haze of champagne bubbles! What came out of the kitchen was so brilliant, and we had the greatest of time. Remiro came back, and all the patrons of the restaurant toasted him and the baby. And as quickly as it had filled up, the restaurant emptied, and I think we all had more champagne just to keep going through the evening service.

As the years came and went, and I set out at various times to explore the world, there was always a job for me at Il Casino till eventually I knew I had to move on. Dear Remiro, he lived and loved, and carried on building his empire, and knowing everybody and going everywhere. He was made a Cavalier by Italy in recognition of his effort between New Zealand and Italy. He died at the age of 56. I thank him, I love him, and I miss him as do many whom he touched in his far too short but excellent life.

It was during my time at Il Casino that Kay had the opportunity to move to the US and do business there for six months with the possibility of longer. I saw a chance to travel and revisit Canada, so I worked hard to save enough money as possible to pay my way. So in September of 1978, we flew out of New Zealand on our first overseas adventure together. We flew to LA and then onto Ohio where Kay was to set up shop, so to speak. The first week we spent in a large round hotel in the middle of Columbus. Kay was busy with her work, and so I was left alone to do what

I could. I wasn't quite sure of my role and what I should be doing. I had brought my modeling portfolio with me, thinking I might get some work. I went to an agency, and they told me that I had a cute face (scowl) but needed a green card to work. So having no luck there, I didn't pursue it.

We moved into a complex, which was like an apartment village with its variety of shops, apartments, cafes, food halls and gym. I tried to get some work but to no avail. I was getting bored. Kay was spending more time away with her work, and so my life started to get rather tedious. I was earning nothing, and my hard-earned savings were running out. I spent time hanging around the apartment watching the soaps, going to the gym, and sleeping.

Even though the place must have been home to hundreds, I rarely saw anyone, so it was difficult to strike up friendships. I spent a bit of time at the gym but was usually the only one there. Next door was this guy whom I had struck up the odd conversation with, and one night he had invited me to come over and watch the football game. We had a few beers, and he started to talk about things he had done in his life and that men of our age had experienced, etc. Men of our age? I asked him how old he thought I was. He looked hard at me and then announced about twenty-eight, same as him. I laughed and as it happened to be my birthday that day, I told him that I had just turned nineteen. I've never seen anyone fall off a chair in shock, and the look on his face was a real Kodak moment. I wasn't sure if I should have been insulted or pleased that he thought me twenty-eight. I could see his brain working all over the place, and I could feel his energy change like a switch had been flicked. It must have been way too much for him as after that, I only had the cursory nod from him if we ever crossed each other's paths.

I did make a friend of a woman called Lyn who worked in the office of the complex, and who also lived there as well. I took to dropping in on her at the office to have a coffee and a chat and just chill out. One day I had this brilliant idea that I needed to have some "wave" in my fairly straight hair, and so Lyn and I had a chat about this. She said she could do it for me as she did heaps of her friends' hair, and it turned out amazing. One afternoon I went to her apartment with the home perm kit I had bought at the supermarket, and as she styled, we watched TV and ate some food and generally laughed our way through the afternoon.

It was decided that after about an hour that I was probably done, and she took out the rollers. As she was unrolling I looked at her face that was sort of blank and she said "OH" in such a way that did not fill me with confidence. My original intent was to have a nice bouncy wave in the front and sides, and as Lyn held the mirror up in front of me I realized why she had said, "OH!" in such a manner.

All along the front and down the sides were tight little rows of curls. I could have auditioned for the lead female role in "Pride and Prejudice."

I started to laugh and thought, "Hell's bells! Kay's going to slaughter me!"

Lyn started to laugh as well and in no time we were on the floor in hysterics. I rushed back to the apartment and straight away into the shower in the hope that I would be able to "wash away" some of the damage, but it was no good. It had set good and proper, and so I sat on the toilet seat and contemplated what my next move would be.

There was none. It was hopeless, and I would have to take my medicine like a man. Kay had been away on business, and I heard the key in the door. I had put the chain up, and so I wrapped a towel around my head—like that's going to make a big difference—and went to open the door. I greeted Kay in that over-friendly-nice-to-see-you-I've-been-a-complete-idiot-but-don't-know-how-to-tell-you voice that men have perfected over the centuries. She was glad to see me and after about four hours asked me why I had a towel around my head.

Words are useless at times, and I think there was enough evidence on my head to say it all, so I took the towel off my head and waited.

Kay stared for a moment as if taking it all in and then burst into fits of laughter.

After a few words of explanation we came to the conclusion that nothing could be done apart from cutting off the most offensive of the curls and letting the rest grow out. So this we proceeded to do, and it wouldn't have been so bad really, but I was heading up to Canada the following week to live and work for a while, and so I was going to make my first appearance in eight years to my relations, looking like some Shirley Temple reject!

I had made the decision to go up to Canada and a cousin had offered me a job in one of his shoe stores and said I could stay with him and his wife until I got settled, so I was able to walk right into employment and not feel the pressure of having to find a place to live. Leaving Kay behind in the US was not easy, and there were a few tears shed in the days that led up to my departure. There was no other choice as Kay was away so much, and I was getting bored and lazy so I had to do something.

So yet another move, and I looked back and realized that in just a little over a year I had formed an important relationship, left school, and been kicked out of home. I had become distanced from my family, established myself in a job that I really liked, created good connections with people I valued, moved offshore and basically grown heaps! Not bad, considering that when I was in that "death room," I had no idea at all where I stood and where I was going.

It had been eight years since I had left Canada, and so on return I had no sense of Canada being my home. Too much had happened to me in New Zealand that had formed my ideas and feelings about myself and the world, and I felt more like a Kiwi than I did a Canadian. And so when I once again stepped onto Canadian soil, I felt like I was a stranger in a new land.

I stayed with my cousin for the first few weeks in Canada and then found an apartment of my own in Vancouver. My first apartment! I was thrilled, excited and totally terrified. This was really it! I was on my own in the world and responsible for myself. I settled into my job, started to make friends and had a life. No big dramas here, just the everyday existence that comes with anyone surviving in the world we all live in. I joined the Vancouver Repertory and went to parties and got to know Vancouver as a nineteen-year-old in 1979.

Most weekends I would take the bus to White Rock where my Nana lived and would stay the weekend, loving her and hanging out. She was a wonderful person, and I always loved her dearly. I'm so glad that I was able to see her as an adult. As a child staying with her, part of her nightly ritual was to gargle and rinse with Listerine and then on the way to bed she would come and give me a kiss and hug goodnight. She still had the same routine all those years later, and to this day I always associate the smell of Listerine with my Nana. I'm not sure what she would think about that!

I wasn't sure how long I was going to stay in Canada and so lived a day-to-day existence. I didn't bother having the phone connected, so any calls I made were from the payphone down the road. This was before the days of mobile phones, of course. I would ring up Kay every night in Ohio if she was there, and we would talk and afterwards I felt flat and wondered what I was doing in Canada when I really wanted to be with her. There was a bit of a tug of war going on emotionally, and then something happened to once again sow a seed of change.

My cousin had a friend who was very psychic, and she had been at my cousin's place for dinner. There was a candle on the table, and as they were talking the candle began to flare up quite high, and Margaret started to get messages from spirit. Amongst other things spirit told her was that I would be returning to the US to be with Kay as there were things that needed to be done.

Kay was going back to New Zealand for Christmas but was going to make a trip up to see me first. It was so good to see her, and we fitted naturally into each other's energy as if it had only been a day or two since we had parted. While she was there, I really started thinking about how much I wanted to be back in the US with her and thought a lot about what the spirits had said through Margaret even though I was unsure about what the "things to be done" were.

Kay went off back to New Zealand and the US, and I saw Christmas out in Vancouver and heralded in the 1980s at a party at the Rep Theatre. It was fancy dress, and I went as an alien, dressed in black and silver. Black velvet jeans, silver shirt, I sprayed my hair silver and glued on false nails and painted them silver, which was a BIG MISTAKE! Think trying to have a pee!

After the New Year I started to get unsettled and drifty and felt I was wasting my time in Canada and needed to make a choice about where to go from there. My calls to Kay were becoming more frequent, and though she wasn't asking me outright to come back, I could feel it in her energy and hear in her voice that's what she wanted me to do, and so I finally made the decision to go back to the US.

Two days before I was leaving, some friends gathered a group together for a farewell dinner at a local Italian place. From there we went to a local club and danced till 4am. The next day I was to spend cleaning up the apartment and then spend my last night in Vancouver at my Nana's place. And the apartment would have been cleaned if I had not spent most of the night making excellent friends with the toilet bowl. The Bolognese I had consumed the night before was at war with my body, and I spent most of that day trying to make a peace pact, but it was better to let the battle fight itself out. Perhaps I was symbolically spewing out all that had occurred over the last year and clearing the way for the future. Or perhaps it was just bad food! I did manage to drag myself around and clean up the place. My cousin arrived and gave me a hand and then drove me to Nana's. Goodbye, apartment! Goodbye, Canada.

The trip back was memorable for two things. Customs were suspicious of my going to the US with no return ticket and almost didn't allow me to go through. And on the plane they served Lobster Newburg and in my post-food poisoning state, I could feel an encore of the night before building up as they placed the pink gluggy mass of shellfish before me, Ugh!

So it was a rather pale and thinner me that Kay greeted at Columbus Airport, and we settled into life together. Kay at this point was getting ready to relocate to the West Coast and two of her relations from New Zealand were to join us as we drove from Ohio to San Francisco in a very indirect path heading east in a recently bought Bedford van. I love the diversity of the US, I love its extremes and its simplicity and its spirituality. As we drove from Ohio east to Virginia, there was a big storm following us that was far from being a tropical one. We spent the first night camped in the van in a truck stop, one small van parked in between giant trucks.

We drove from there on to Washington to stay with one of Kay's former bridesmaids. The van was parked outside the house, and Kay and family stayed indoors while I had drawn the short straw and had to sleep in the van. The first night there was a heavy snowfall, but I managed to keep warm, despite the snow piling up around the van! The next day we went to visit the Lincoln Memorial, and I recall thinking what an austere building for an austere man. From there it was west to Carolina and then southeast to Georgia where we went to the Peach Tree Centre in Atlanta with its glass elevator on the outside of the building. I thought I would be smart and get in first to get the view. As people piled in, I was literally pressed against the glass of the elevator with only a couple of inches of glass, separating me from my human nature and the realms of divinity! As we soared up into the clouds, I thought of the scene in the movie "Towering Inferno" when the glass was sucked out and so was a woman!

From Georgia we headed west toward New Orleans. In Alabama, we drove across a very long bridge, and Queen was on the radio singing "This Thing Called Love." There were small speed bumps on the road, and as we went over them, the van seemed to keep in beat with the song. A hurricane had just been through the area and though it wasn't bad, the place was almost deserted, and it was a bit weird driving through Mobile with not a soul to be seen. Carolina, Georgia, Alabama, Louisiana, Texas, New Mexico, Arizona—we drove through them all and experienced America in all its glory.

We went to Juarez, Mexico, and walked through the dusty streets looking at all the stalls and goods for sale. In one stall we bought a beautiful woolen Mexican rug from a woman called Elvira. She was very tall with a long face and had two big spots of rouge plastered on her golden cheeks. The colour contrasted too much with her complexion, making her look like an overly made-up doll. She also carried a little dog with her way before Paris Hilton did; in fact, Paris Hilton wasn't even born then! I liked Elvira very much. She was very nice, and we chatted with her for a long time. She was very interested to hear where we came from and who we were. At one point she asked Kay how old she was and was astonished when Kay told her. She could not believe how young she looked.

"How do you stay so young" Elvira asked.

Kay mentioned that she drank lots of tea called Amber Tips, and Elvira eagerly wrote the name down, hoping, I think, to find the fountain of youth in a cup of tea!

We drove on to San Francisco, and the plan was that Kay and I would settle there, and her family would return to New Zealand. Kay decided though that she had done all she wanted to do in the US with her job, and so it was the four of us who boarded the plane in LA back to New Zealand. A couple of years later, I was working in San Francisco and was staying at the Hilton. As I looked out the window at the vista below me, I spotted the area where in 1979 we had camped. I wonder what my reaction would have been if someone had said to me in 1979 that I would be working there thirty years later as a spiritual channel. I probably would have just looked blank!

By the time we returned to New Zealand, my Shirley Temple curls had grown out, and I had at last achieved the wave that I wanted in my hair. I had also grown my first "beard" and looked a bit hippy and Californian. The look worked well for me as on my return I went back to the modeling agency I had been at, and they cast me for an ad in the paper, for all things, advertising Bedford Vans. I went back to Il Casino and fell easily back into New Zealand life. From nineteen till my early twenties, I stayed in the hospitality business even leasing a small pizza/pasta restaurant from Remiro. It was called Guido's and Kay and I worked together side-by-side, twelve hours a day, seven days a week. We closed early on Sunday evening and would treat ourselves to a bottle of champagne, which on drinking, we promptly fell asleep watching the Sunday Horror.

I seemed to have the knack for making pasta and could toss the pizza quite high. Even Remiro with all his expertise was impressed by my culinary ability. Again, it felt familiar so I was no doubt calling on some past life in Italy. Remiro had been giving us a hand as we eased our way into the business, and I will never forget the first Saturday night when we did it solo. The whole place suddenly became packed, and I was so inundated with orders that I completely went blank for a moment and had no idea at all what I was doing. I didn't panic at all.

I simply walked into the huge fridge/freezer that was in the shop and closed the door! I sat there for a moment or two, breathing in the cool air while I gathered my thoughts.

A voice in my head then said, "Go out now. You will be okay."

I felt very calm and peaceful, and so I went back out and was brilliant. I tell you, the last place I thought I would get a divine message was in the middle of a fridge/freezer!

Actually that freezer came in handy on another occasion. Our local shopkeeper, who was from Croatia, was having a party, and we were invited. We went along and in those days my drink was scotch and soda. My host presented me with a highball, rather strong, which I slowly sipped all night. It was a great night of conversation and laughter and without realizing it, my host had been topping up my drink and so when we got up to go home, the room was swaying. As the night air hit me, it got worse and so once again, I was making excellent friends with a toilet bowl!

The next day was Sunday, and I had to go into the restaurant to do food prep for that night. Every ten minutes or so, I would have to walk into the freezer, breath in lungs full of cold air, clear my head and go back to work. To this day, I have never touched scotch!

We stayed in that restaurant till November 1981, and then Kay and I decided to move to Melbourne in Australia. We shut up our flat, found someone to take over the lease to the restaurant, and once again went off on an adventure. I found a job in a clothing shop and then later as a cook in a small all-night café. I loved Australia, but it was tough to get established and so in the early part of 1982, we went back to New Zealand. I was getting sick of the restaurant business and the night hours but stuck it out for a little longer. I felt really restless and often had this feeling that I should be doing something else, but had no idea what that might be. I was twenty-one and had packed a great deal into my life since I was eighteen. I wanted to grow and expand more but really had no idea what direction to take. The ever-growing feeling that someone or something was trying to tell me something kept coming up, and it made me feel that I had to make some choices. At this point in life I did not relate this to any "spiritual message" or anything of that nature. I knew that there was *more*, but more of what, and how did I get it?

At times I felt that Kay and I were not growing together in a way that was good for us, and twice I had left the relationship but always within a matter of weeks, we were back together. What was the pull that kept us linked? What were we heading towards in our future? There was a time when I really had decided that we had no future, and I needed to go. On that day, Kay's Mother had a heart attack, and we went up together to see her in Auckland, and this once again pulled us together.

Something was saying to me, "You have to stay, there is something you have to see through, something you have to do together."

This feeling was so compelling, and it was so confusing as I had so many mixed feelings about everything. And so as her mother recovered, we went back to Wellington and back to an uncertain future.

Wherever you stand in life, the rest of your life and its futures are always there for you as infinite possibilities. It is rather like a moving montage, always altering as you edit the outcomes by your ever-changing thoughts and experiences. How far you choose to reach is entirely up to you, but I believe that as you become proficient in positioning yourself appropriately, you always have within easy reach all that you need to be successful in your life. This proficiency is essential to your whole well-being, and it comes about by your involvement in the present.

The energy of the present can be seen as a magnet where all points of life will converge as one. I see a picture of a human being standing, and billions of lines of light are being directed to this being. As the lines of light flow into the being, they assimilate as one point of light, as "creation energy." From this point the being unconsciously categorizes this energy and then sends it out of itself by transmission. If you are standing consciously as your God Energy, then the signals that you transmit create a positive proficiency, enabling you, the being, to establish the appropriate links with the "success energy."

The present is the point where all life converges as one point of light.

As your higher nature directs you through your life, it's essential to remember that your higher nature is always working in your best interests. It knows you, about you and all your intentions for this lifetime, and it will forever dip into the cornucopia of you to see where you have decided to head.

Your higher nature will never be distracted by your human nature, and as your human nature keeps changing the route all the time, the higher nature simply pauses and configures the best route to take you to your positive place of destination. It's rather like a GPS system. You may have programmed it to take you to your destination, but you may turn away from the plan as you have seen something that has grabbed your interest. The GPS will automatically reconfigure the best route to take you back to the road to ensure you get to your destination. Until you program a new destination, it will keep coming up with a new plan, and this is what your higher nature does, and it does it better when it knows you have considered the present as the higher nature will use the power of the present to propel you to your positive outcomes. People have often spoken of the feeling of having a guardian angel within, and this is your higher nature. I find it interesting that human nature will not at times listen to their true nature and instead prefer to put their faith in sources that they believe to be more informed than they are.

It's impossible not to be informed as you were given all the information before you were born, and its higher natures wish that you follow the information that is given for you to excel in the way that you were programmed. And yet life on Earth is full of distractions that seem to take you away from the present and lock you into the past or the future. Your intentions to stay present can be sorely tried time and time again, creating despair and frustration, and it's this very despair and frustration that are important to pay attention to.

What they are showing you is not what you are doing wrong, but they are indicators to you that you are not aligned with the present and not engaged in a relationship with your higher nature. They are for all intents and purposes warning you that you are off track. The more you stay off track, the warnings get bigger until you eventually stop getting warnings, and instead, you create some sort of event in your life that stops you in your tracks and needs your absolute attention to remedy the situation. This doesn't mean that you no longer have the connection with your higher nature. What happens is that higher nature has seen that you have made a choice that has taken you in a certain direction. Having observed carefully the direction you are going, it then starts to inform you through instinct and thoughts of the best actions to take to bring about harmony.

Higher nature is always on the look-out for you. Your higher nature is connected to source power and also receives information from other forms of guidance that you work with.

In a way you all have a team that is there for you. Let's call it your own personal "council." From the moment that you incarnate, you are never alone. For a start you are all source energy in every way that it is expressed in physical and non-physical forms. Being this collective energy ensures that you are being carried in the stream of great love throughout all eternity.

As was written previously, when you make the choice to reincarnate you are given council and guidance by spirit to assist you in creating the choices that will best serve the life you are establishing. The spirits that assist you in this process will more than likely become part of your own personal council. This council is always in direct contact with your higher nature, and it is this council that you receive most of your messages from. Making a link with your higher nature is also making a link with the council, as one cannot have one without the other. The same applies when you are affirming your God nature. The moment you do that, you are opening up all channels of energy that links you with all source energy and whatever forms the energy takes. When you are being present, you are standing in a place that allows an alignment to occur with all source power and all forms of guidance that you wish to be conscious of.

Note that I have said, "You wish to be conscious of." Though all may be with you always, it is still from your own direct invitation that you allow assistance to be given. There is nothing that can come unto you without your specific invitation and creating from the power point of the present, engages you in conscious intention. Every intention has its own unique code, and once the code is put in place through your desire, it makes a link with the precise form of guidance that is pertinent to that desire. It's rather like you are the team leader, and you are informing your team what positions they have to take and what roles you delegate them. The "team," of course, has opinions and suggestions to make; after all the team is well-trained in understanding you and your situations. When it comes to putting together a team, you don't just go for any old energy. You go to the ultimate pool of higher energy that has a total understanding of you and your issues.

The Guiding Forces

All living energy is surrounded by guiding forces throughout life. It is factually impossible for life not to be guided, as the links to all life force are a natural part of living. When people come to consult with me, a question that is often asked is "Who are my Guides?" Let's talk about this now and give you some insights about this and how to work with this energy that is forever prevalent in life. One major point to accept straight away is this:

You Are All the Guiding Force.

How can you not all be the guiding force when you are all the God energy? If you can accept this concept and live this, you have then consciously forged the connection with source power, consequently opening up all the channels of information to use at your leisure. It's rather like logging into your computer so you can access all the information that you have downloaded. In this case the password is *I AM GOD!* Once you are logged in, you can then surf the web of cosmic consciousness to fulfil your soul's desire! Having logged in, all of source energy will note that you are online and will await your instructions. These instructions are sent by you through your thoughts and actions and, of course, the vibrations that you are emitting. When you Skype, you are able to see your contacts and who is online. When you have turned on "conscious awareness," your whole being turns on a light, therefore, showing all consciousness you are ready to receive.

As a spiritual being, you are constantly online. In fact, it's out of the question that you would ever log off! As human beings, you seem to be in a state of logging on and off all through the day and all through your lives. The guides from source energy are there to ensure that when you drop the links, you get the reminders to pick them up again.

It's best to define guides as a *"guiding force"* that will manifest itself throughout your life in myriad ways. You only have to be aware of what's happening around you in life to see how much you are being guided by life's events and the events of people around you. For this reason the need to pay attention to the energy of the day, and how you are responding to this energy is essential to your ability to *read the signs*. Too often people will seek *beyond themselves* before they look at what is around them. People do that because they are at times not validating their soul as their true nature, and the assistance they seek has to do with their human nature.

When you seek guidance, ask for it from your soul and for your soul, not your human nature.

The soul will take the guidance, and it will direct it through the human nature by the way the soul will lead.

You are a God on Earth, and the first place you should always look when you are looking for solutions and guidance is exactly where you are. It is not feasible to think that the God force would create anything that did not have access to source energy. Wherever you go, whatever planet you are on, and whatever dimension you are participating in, you will find everything you need. So before you look outside self and beyond this world look at, to quote a phrase, "What is as plain as the nose on your face."

Where you stand right now is where you will find everything you need.

As I mentioned before, you are linked always with your own higher nature, and this nature has your best interests in sight all the time. The information that higher nature gives you is often sourced from your own "bank of experience" that you carry in soul. It accesses data given by your "council" and sends this data to you through ideas and feelings. Communication with your personal council is as fun as it is affirmative. I have often through a meditation connected people with their council, and without fail every person meets their council in a specific place. Now the place that you meet your council may not be what you expect.

One woman met her council in a barn full of hay bales. Everyone was dressed in jeans and boots, and they all sat on the bales and discussed the issues of her life. Another person found himself in an ice-cream parlour with all his council sitting on red leather revolving seats eating ice-cream sundaes. I did laugh when I took Blair to meet his council; they were all at the top floor of a big glass tower. There were comfortable leather sofas and glass and chrome, everyone was wearing an Armani suit!

Having organized a meeting with your council doesn't just sit there and wait for them to talk. Greet them and give them a hug and ask them pertinent questions relating to the life you are living. Be very present, as council understands the relevance of informing you of what's happening NOW. If needed, it will always guide you towards the past or some future possibility, but it will only do this if it feels it is needed. Be specific in your questions and needs, and once you get the information then, always thank them with gratitude. Take the information and then weave it into your life. If you don't do this, council will remind you in your next meeting, and it will not pass on any unnecessary information to you particularly when you haven't used what they suggested before. And always remember that your council is with you from the very moment you create your deals whilst you are still in spirit till the time when you finish this life.

The spirits of people you have known in this life, of course, guide you. The relationships that you have with people while they are alive don't necessarily finish when these people pass into spirit. These are souls that you have had many, many lifetimes with and so the connection you have forged throughout your history together builds a familiarity of energy. You will always recognize each other's vibrations and be drawn to each other, assisting, guiding, loving and helping each other to create a better way of being.

You will draw guidance from the lives and teachings of master teachers that you feel drawn towards. They may strike a note in you that is important to pursue, as there is obviously something vital for you to learn. This is why through your lifetime you may choose to follow the beliefs and teachings of a particular master teacher or spiritual leader. Some years ago this question was asked of me at a meeting: "Tabaash, how is it that you may have several different teachers, each with different opinions on the same subject? Who are you to believe?"

I replied, "In your life you will travel down many diverse roads, and each road will present to you a different way of looking at your journey. It is the same with teachers. They present themselves to you by your invitation and show you an assortment of perspectives. What you resonate to is the one that you should look at. Invariably at the end of the day, each is not presenting to you any answer but rather awakening something in you that allows you to create what you know is best for you at that time. This fits in particularly with what I have said about there being many futures."

You are forever dipping into the collective of life's energy to propel you towards the best outcomes. As you emit the energy of your thoughts, actions and feelings, source power as a collective is aware and endeavouring to guide you into and, of course, away from situations that may not be beneficial to you. That is when you get a particular feeling about doing something or conversely not acting upon something. Not following this has proved fatal and counter-productive for some, and for others it has saved or improved their lives.

God does speak to you all, and it's always loud and clear. God isn't a big voice in your head or ears; God speaks to you through life. And so when you align yourself with the idea of your God nature, then you have all the stations on all the time. Your own authentic self knows how to listen to the station that best serves you. Life is turned on all the time, and it's you, first and foremost, that defines if you hear clearly what you need or if you are just hearing one big noise!

CHAPTER NINE

Your dreams are your dreams because of all the other dreams you have ever engaged in.

Spirit

Relationships really are like running a business; you need to profit from them, and to achieve that, you have to be careful about the way you invest in them. To ensure you invest well, you have to have a good investment in yourself as an individual. One of the collective lessons we are all learning on Earth is about how we all relate to each other. Relationships on all levels seem to be one of the foremost ways of developing ourselves. From the time we draw our very first breath till the very last, we are establishing innumerable connections with people, events, ideas, sensations and so forth. These are all ways of relating to the world that teach us how we are all relating to ourselves. Many people believe that what's happening around them is independent of them, and personally has nothing to do with them. So many of us are discovering that what's occurring in the world is *because* of who we are, what we think, etc. I really resonated to what Gregg Braden said in his book, *The Spontaneous Healing of Belief.*

We are experiencing what we are creating, but we are also creating what we are experiencing.

Put this concept into the dynamics of a relationship, and it rather changes the view. Take responsibility for your relationships and know that those are the choices that you have made to promote your well-being in all ways. You can see your love affairs, parental relationships, siblings, friends, etc., all in a different light because you then stop humanizing them and instead spiritualize them. Doing this gives you access to the true intention of that relationship which was forged before the human nature got in the way.

In my early twenties I was expanding my idea of myself and wanted to be more, do more, and shake off the vibrations of the past. It was really difficult for me though as I had a lot of fear that I would get it all wrong. I was fearful of being criticized and put down and also feared that I *would* get it right, and then I wouldn't know how to sustain what I had created. Then there was the fear that I would upset someone or everyone and everything, so it was obvious that fear was one of my major karmic issues! There is a phrase I read somewhere about fear that put it all into perspective.

If you focus too much on fear, then you will simply attract to you the very things that you are afraid of.

Now how true is that!

Even now there is not a day that goes by that I haven't felt fear. As Tabaash has taught me though, I don't have to spend a whole lot of time ridding myself of fear or even understanding it. Rather as I grow through my experiences in life, I learn how to manage the energy of my fear. And the best place to manage that energy is a place where you feel your God nature, and I have found that regardless of the relationships that I am involved in, when I am my "authentic self," then I realize the importance of standing alone. That is applicable to all of us though many may not choose to look at that concept in this life. Of course, standing alone does not mean being alone; it means that you have made yourself responsible for everything about you and the life that you are living. You cannot and will not make anyone else accountable for the life you are living.

Whilst growing up and feeling a sense of isolation and non-acceptance by my peers, I suppose I was teaching myself about being alone, and that does tend to make you more aware of yourself! I think standing alone makes a great deal of sense as it seems to me to be a very honest place to be. From that place I believe you seems to be able to "hear more" as you don't have the disturbances of other people's energies to distract you. I think of all those people through history who have isolated themselves at times, and by doing so, they have been able to come up with something brilliant in the fields of science, art, intellect. If they had not taken a sabbatical from life at times, then perhaps they would never had created the inroads they had? I believe we all have to step off the field now and then, and by doing so, it connects us with the parts of us that have those higher ideas.

By doing this, it allows us to see our personal relationship with our own formula of life and helps us determine industrious changes that we can bring about. It's a place that shows us how we are living. Are we living to the best of what we have decided to be? As we become more involved in our self-development, the importance of such a concept becomes more evident. It's all very well to know, but are we living what we know? Through living our beliefs, we then truly acknowledge that we are wise.

After coming back from Melbourne in 1982, I went back to working at IL Casino. Remiro had bought the building next door and expanded the restaurant to establish a great eating institution, and for a while, my working there seemed to be a good thing to do. Then something strange started to happen.

Within minutes of arriving at work, I would throw up, and I always threw up three times. After the third time, it would stop, and I would be able to carry on with the evening. I thought I must have picked up some sort of bug or had eaten something dodgy, but it kept happening, and then I twigged that this wasn't about food or a bug. This was my body saying something to me. When I got that, I realized that it was time for me to leave IL Casino for good. I made the decision to leave and having made that decision, I stopped being sick. I realized I must have thrown up once for mind, once for body, and once for spirit!

I stayed in hospitality for a little longer, but I really had lost my appetite for that life style and type of work. I toyed with the idea of studying at the university but could not make a choice and wasn't sure whether I wanted to dedicate myself to years of study at that stage in my life.

Kay and I had left the apartment where we had started our lives together and had bought an old house built in 1860 that we both admired. It had been converted into two flats in the 1920s. The house was in a suburb called Mount Victoria and was just on the outskirts of the city. Oriental Bay Beach was five minutes' walk from the sunny and charming house even though it needed a great deal of work. The house wasn't even on the market, and so we approached an agent with an offer. To make a long story short, all those spirit energies were obviously making some plans for our future with their cunning "let's influence" front. Within weeks we had purchased the property that for the last 36 years now has been our home and my place of work.

I find it interesting that when we went to view the property, the tenant in the flat downstairs wouldn't let us in to look as they were annoyed that it was going to be sold. So the first we actually saw of the property was not where we were to live but the upstairs flat that I was eventually to use as my consultancy rooms as the channel for Tabaash. Also, some years ago Kay had been at a conference at the hotel across the road and had always looked at the house thinking how wonderful it would be to live in that house!

From the moment we moved in, we started to renovate the house. At one point we had pulled off all the old interior dusty rotted wood walls and had a huge pile of ancient wood up to the ceiling in the living room. It was winter, and so we "literally" burnt up the house in the old fireplace. The kitchen was an old lean-to, built on the back of the house in the 1880s and even had an old 1920s fridge in working order and a stove from the same era. The toilet was just off the kitchen and was no bigger than a small cupboard. There were gaps in the wooden walls where plants were growing through. It was a very cold quick trip to the dunny if you wanted it in the middle of the night.

We worked hard getting the house to a more liveable state, and it became a total vocation for both of us to make it the best we could. We rented the upstairs flat out and lived downstairs. I was very fortunate to be co-habiting with a rather skilled and attractive carpenter called Kay. The woman was a marvel, and over the years her carpentry skills have amazed me. I came home from work one day to discover a wall and doorway that had been in the hallway in the morning weren't there in the afternoon!

All of us have natural abilities that we know we are good at and, of course, recognize the things that we should just simply stay away from! Kay was a natural carpenter; I was good at concreting and plastering and painting. As a team we worked well together, and we settled into our home and routines and our life together. And then an event occurred that once more would change the way I saw and experienced life.

One night in May we were in bead, and Kay suddenly sat up in bed, and said aloud, "What's that?"

She took my hand and led it to her right breast, and I felt a rather hard large lump. I wasn't familiar with the concepts of breast cancer, but as the months unfolded, we both became experts.

Kay got an appointment with her GP the next day and in a sort of jolly voice he announced, "Yes, I am pretty sure in is a tumour."

Then in a very matter of fact manner, he started organizing biopsies and appointments with cancer specialists. The news was not good, and we had a few very bad days as we let this news sink in.

On June 8th, Kay's birthday, she underwent a mastectomy of the right breast. The cancer had spread to the lymph nodes under the right arms, and so they were also removed. Just how significant is having major surgery on your birthday? While Kay was in surgery, I sat in her hospital room and several hours later, she was wheeled in looking very pale.

I remember I brushed her hair for her while she was asleep. The prospects were not good, and so we prepared ourselves for what needed to be done in regards to treatment. This was bad, but we both had a strong feeling that she would not die from this.

Here is a great example of the determination and strength my wife has. The day she came out of hospital we went home, and she went straight to the garden shed and got out a shovel. We were in the process of building a new fence up one side of the property, and there were plenty of fence postholes to dig.

With a drain still attached to her surgery wound, Kay dug a few shovelfuls of dirt, then handed me the shovel, and told me to finish. She was making a statement in that action in regards to how she wanted to deal with all of this. She did what she had to do and simply got on with life. Our life then evolved around Kay's trips to the hospital for her chemotherapy and getting on with life as normally as we could.

My wife has always been a strong-minded individual who liked to do the driving, and so suddenly here she was in a position where I had to do the driving, and I have to admit I was a bit unsure of what I was supposed to do. I had to grow up very fast and once again redefine life and the roles I had to play. All our lives are so full of catalysts that are indicators that changes have to be made. These changes make us think more deeply and observe more carefully the circumstances we find ourselves involved in.

"Listen to the whispers of life," says Tabaash.

And if we don't hear the whispers or pay attention to them, they get louder and louder until we have created something that we can't ignore. It's unfortunate for us in our human nature's tendency to wait until we physically hurt before we often do something about listening. Kay's cancer for us was a wake-up call, telling us to pay attention to life in a new way.

The way I look at all of this now is that we fitted her cancer into our life rather than let it overwhelm us. There were never any big discussions, no deep and meaningful soul-searching moments that spoke of great and profound things to us. There were no big promises or major agreements. We allowed the experience to flow into our lives, and we adapted as we needed to. No need for dramas, or no crying on anybody's shoulders. It just became a part of us until it was no longer there.

I took a photo of Kay after all her hair and eyebrows and eyelashes fell out. Devoid of any makeup, she could have been a man or a woman. There used to be a BBC program on the telly called *Steptoe and Son*. Kay could make a face like the old man Steptoe and with no hair or makeup, she looked exactly like him, and it cracked me up every time.

When I had been a volunteer at hospice, I found it interesting that in that pre-death stage so many of the patients became in their physical appearance quite androgynous, a state we are like when we are first born. We come as God and then in life, we developed the human character that will define that lifetime. When we have finished our lives, we shake off that human nature and go back to being God.

As Kay progressed with her chemotherapy, the veins on her hands started to get irritated by the treatment. Usually a needle would be placed in one of the veins on her hands, and that's where the chemo would be administered. In Kay's case they could no longer do this, so she had to have a Hickman Catheter placed through the neck and out through the chest. This enabled the chemo a direct link to her bloodstream. It so awful had to see her go through all of this. She had to make sure that the tube was always sterile and had to drain daily fluid from the body and put saline solution in to keep it clean. She did all of this herself. Just after she got out of hospital after having the catheter put in, a district nurse came over to make sure Kay was following the sterile process accurately.

She had drained off the fluid and had placed it in a small bowl. We heard this slurp sound, and we all turned to see our dog, a

Cavalier King Charles licking her lips as she devoured what had been in the bowl!

We went up to the hospital for her chemo and, of course, got to know other patients and their families. We were all on a similar journey, and so it all pulled us together as an odd assorted family. Everybody seemed all rather matter of fact about what we were all doing there, and I expect that under the circumstances that was the best approach to take.

There was one man that I will always remember who had a brain tumour. His wife had put him on a macrobiotic diet, and she was adamant that this would work for him and cure him. The very first time I met him the idea that he was going to die came straight to my thoughts. I felt that part of him had already departed, and that this was the final last-ditch effort, but quite frankly you could see he just did not have it in him to live anymore. We got to know his wife and him quite well, and it broke my heart when I watched him force down another glass of wheatgrass juice when I knew that he wanted to wolf down a Big Mac and fries. His wife was most insistent that he continued this diet, and I knew that everything he was doing he was doing because she was afraid of his death, and she was trying to do everything in her power to stop it from happening. He knew though. He knew that he was going to die, and yet for her he kept playing the game. He did die, and I often wonder if she was ever racked with guilt. Did she ever think during that time of what he wanted, or was she so consumed about what she wanted?

I've seen this a lot over the years—people who find it difficult to accept that a loved one will die. They seek out every possible cure and potion and lotion, etc., in the hope that it will cure the afflicted person. Some get so desperate in the hope that they will find "the cure" that they hop from one thing to another instead of accepting that the sickness and death of their loved one is what it is. Now, of course, I'm not saying that one should not do everything one feasibly can do, but there are times when it is obvious that the illness is terminal. I think that's when you should look at the quality of life and sharing you can have with that person rather than put pressure on yourself and him/her. Looking back on that couple we got to know, I feel sad for her because she denied herself and her husband a time of sharing and caring when that was most essential. She literally fought for his life till the end, and at the end she was exhausted.

Kay made her own choices and ultimately listened to her body and what it was wanting. One day I came home from work, and she was sitting at the table eating the most enormous plate of silver-beet I had ever seen. She said her body was telling her to eat it. Another time I came home, and she had just gotten back from a chemo session. At times these sessions made her rather constipated, and she had taken some laxative to get things flowing, so to speak. I found her sitting on the toilet, the television in front of her, watching and waiting for things to take effect. I nearly peed myself laughing!

Before all her hair fell out, these wonderful girlfriends she had come around with bottles of champagne, and they sat in our living room drinking bubblies and plaiting Kay's long hair into little plaits. I stayed in the kitchen and made tea and coffee. Her hair fell out not long after that. The people I loved the most during that time were the ones who simply fitted into our situation and got on with the usual business of living as if Kay's cancer was simply a little bump in the road and easy to get over.

And then there were those who just did not know what to do or what to say or how to cope, so they never came, and we never usually saw them again. That was fine with me, as I didn't want people like that around anyway. Obviously people deal with other people's traumas in different ways. To some, the thought of a terminal illness must bring up a great fear and other varied emotions they can't cope with. To others, it seems a great embarrassment, as they really have no idea of how to be in those situations. We really do teach other a great deal of life, don't we? By the way that we all respond to each other and our situations.

I wish more people could understand that the best lessons in life are the ones we give each other by simply living life in the ways we do. I have heard so many say that they have done nothing to make a difference in the world and to others. As Tabaash has said, "Your message to the world is simply the life that you are living." I suppose most think that they have to do something that makes some grand statement or become some great philanthropist or find a cure for some illness, etc. Knowing your God nature as your true nature is, of course, the simplest way to make a difference. Then from there you build and see what more is possible for you to do. This is all, of course, relative to the life you are living and its circumstances. One can only do what is possible after all.

As the months went by, we just got on living, and we started to be drawn towards reading spiritual books about life and death. I was managing a clothing store at this stage, and there was a New Age bookstore two shops down from where I worked. I would go in there and peruse the shelves for anything that grabbed me. Next to the bookstore was a small deli where I would buy bagels and port salute cheese. I would take my books and my smelly cheese and find a little sunny place to munch and eat in my lunchtime.

Kay and I started meditation, and Kay would occasionally get some spiritual healing from a man called Ray who worked on the wharf. He was this astoundingly gifted gentle Maori man who had a group of other healers around them, and he became a good friend. Life was opening up in a new way that was familiar to me—yet at the same time all brand new. I could feel the "something more" I had known as a child, and for the first time in this life, I started to actively pursue it.

So in our need to gain "the light," we immersed ourselves in anything that we could. We attended Japanese Buddhist meetings where we were all crammed into a small room, where we chanted till we were hoarse and dizzy. We sat in Hare Krishna meetings where we did more chanting and then ate wonderful food. I stared into crystals until I was cross-eyed, gazed at the flame of a candle in an open-eyed meditation till my eyes were so dry from not blinking that I could hardly close them.

It was hard to get some privacy at home at this stage as we had pretty well torn down all the old walls of the downstairs as we were re-wiring and "re-everythinging"! So I would go into the little garden shed where our dog slept and make myself comfortable and do my meditations. Often this was difficult as Tiffany, the dog, thought I was going up there to give her some loving, and so she would climb up on my lap. I would sit there with my eyes closed trying hard to "find the silent space within" only to open my eyes to find these big brown dog eyes staring intently at me! That just made me laugh and, of course, then she barked and wanted to play. It was too cold and uncomfortable in there anyway, so I gave up the garden shed as a place to find enlightenment and made the most of our temporary open plan living arrangement.

I tried being a vegetarian and drank lots of wheat grass, which always made me throw up, as my stomach did not take to it. We had heard that there were public screenings of channelled material, so we found out where to go and frequented the evenings often. We met like-minded people where we discussed what was happening and how everything was changing. We went to Spiritualist Church meetings where we would sometimes get messages from our guides through mediums, and I read and read anything I could get my hands on. The spiritual kitchen gates had been opened, and I felt ravenous! I was meditating so much that I felt like I was on drugs, that "something more" seemed to be turning into "something is," and it all felt so easy and natural. It was hard to not see the world and everyone I knew in the old way, and so as I absorbed what I was experiencing, subtle changes in the way I felt and participated in the world became evident to me. The familiar energy of consciousness was embracing me and caressing my soul, and I was responding and seeing my authentic self.

And then there was one book that spoke volumes to me and that was *Out on a Limb* by Shirley Maclaine. That book was a major turning point for me. It pulled together all the things that I had always been feeling and gave me the biggest view of my authentic self to date. In that one book was all the "something more." Thank you, Shirley! I will forever be grateful for the courage it took you to write that book, and I'm sure that there are many who feel the same way I do about *Limb*.

Kay was getting better, and I was meditating so much that I was living on several dimensions all at the same time. The job I had in the clothing shop I loved more than anything I had. The shop had its own designer, and the factory was upstairs in the same building. It was the 80s, and the clothes were funky and the music was funky and life was a great Mind, Body, and Spirit party. There were quite a few shops in the same street, and I got to know the people who worked in them really well.

Across the road from the shop I worked in was a café where a few of us would meet every morning before we started work. We would sit up there and drink coffee and smoke our cigarettes. We really formed a little family really, and for as long as we all worked in the area over the years, we always made sure we met up in the morning. We would talk and smoke and be whatever we needed to be—supportive, disgusted or sympathetic about whatever drama was being played out by any of us at the time. I suppose we were a support team for each other and without realizing it, we had become each other's therapists.

There were a group of older women who sat at one of the other tables. Two of them worked for a department store, and the other was a violinist for the New Zealand Symphony. We all became fast friends, and I value to this day the connection that we all had. During this time the husband of one of the women passed away, and I shall never forget the day she re-joined the fold after a short break. We surrounded and protected her like a loving family, and I like to think that we all helped in her healing process.

I was having some off the planet meditations at this stage in my life. One night I was laying on the floor, pillow under my head just going for gold in the relaxation I was feeling. The thought came into my mind to think of the word "God." So I did and then something said, "Think love." I did that and it became a mantra in my head, and I could feel my body moving into a lovely weightless state. I kept repeating this in my head, and the energy of the words seemed to take over something in me, and in an instant I felt this feeling like I was rushing up towards something. I had the impression of two great doors opening in front of me and then the sensation I had was everything beyond Earth and human nature. I felt such bliss and heard my body let out a great long happy sigh, and then I was gone. I had no idea how long I was "out there," but when I came to, my arms were extended out in front of me as if to reach for something or someone, and tears were streaming down my face. The sense of peace was so absolute, and the feeling of great knowing was intact. I looked into the mirror and my face was aglow with light, and my eyes were filled with wisdom that had been lost. It was God and I wanted more.

In *Out on a Limb* there was a passage where David told Shirley that we were all God, and the greatest way to affirm our power was to announce, "I AM GOD." That always resonated to me and from the moment I read that statement, I affirmed it in my thoughts. I said it out loud all the time as often as possible for years and years and years. I got to the point where I was actually dreaming that I was saying, "I AM GOD," and once I even had a dream that I was dreaming that I was saying it. It was obviously sinking through all the layers of me! It just made sense to me, and so I never questioned it or thought, "Yeah, right." I just knew it to be true. And I still do, and everyday all through the day I affirm it in my thoughts and words. It works! Try it!

In 2008 I visited a wonderful dear friend, my darling soul brother Tosh, in the hospital. He had a major infection and was in an induced coma. We almost lost him and while I was there sitting by him, I had a meditation where I went to his spirit and brought him back to his body. I just knew that he wasn't ready to go yet, so naturally I had to do something about it.

When he came out of the coma, he remembered that happening. Thank God he listened to his bro! He was eventually moved from ICU and into a ward, and I was a daily visitor. We were chatting away one afternoon, and this young nurse came into the room.

She looked at Tosh and then she looked at me and then said to Tosh, "Is this your son"? (referring to me)

"It's so nice to see father and son so close."

Tosh and I stared at each other, and then I burst out laughing and said to the nurse, "Actually we are the same age!"

I had just turned forty-eight the week before and Tosh a few months before that, so I suppose he was older than me. Well, that poor nurse was so mortified; she could not get out of the room fast enough. Tosh looked like a man kicked when he was down.

I looked at him and said, "Well, saying and investing in I AM GOD all these years seems to have paid some dividends. Tosh, I'm glad you decided to hang around. The world really needs you, and who you are, and I love you."

I can understand why so being God challenges many. For a start most of us have been brought up to know God as something *apart* from us as opposed to *being us*. Then there is the religious belief as God as something so beyond what we could possibly be and that we have to be ruled and afraid of his wrath. However, at the end of the day being God is really being accountable for what you have created and quite frankly, I think some people find that just a little bit too challenging. Much easier to point the finger at other sources rather than realize you're the one responsible. It's the highest way we can be, the ultimate vibration. We are being faced now with this concept more than at any other time in our history. I believe that many accept this now and are looking at how to bring it into their everyday lives.

We are all co-writers in this new spiritual adventure, and we all have prime roles to play.

And this is what I was feeling as the God in me kept waking me up and challenging my human nature. I recognized in others the same energy and wanted to have kindred spirits around. I was attracting some interesting experiences in my life because of this new energy I was emanating.

One quiet afternoon as I was mulling over quivering vibrational portals (just joking), I was standing by the front window of the shop and saw this woman passing by, look in the shop window at me and then pass on. I didn't think anything of it, and then she came back and into the shop and said to me, "I see all these horses around you, and this signifies your strong spirit and the work that you shall do in the future."

I was rather taken aback and wasn't sure what the best way to reply to this was, and so I made polite murmurs and sounds of interest. We talked for a while and then she left. I have actually met this woman on and off over the years, and boy was she right!

Another time Kay and I and some friends were sitting on the front veranda during summertime having a glass of wine and chatting as we watched people go by. A young guy in his late twenties walked by and looked at us all as he passed by, and about two minutes later, he came back and walked up to me and gave me a little book. He told me he had a feeling to give the book to me, and then he left. I looked down at the book in my hands, and it seemed homemade. As I opened it for further inspection I discovered that it was full of spiritual poems and passages. I was very moved by his gesture but at the same time was wondering what was going on here? Why was this happening to me?

We had been attending a development circle through the Spiritualist Church, and we would meet up with other people where we would have guided meditations and discussions. I loved going to these meetings. They were very relaxed and informative, and it was a good positive group energy. In one of the meditations, I found myself in this long, long room that had a great many books on both sides and the most enormous floor space. I walked and walked or perhaps glided? Anyway, I found myself standing before this giant lectern, the sort you see in big cathedrals. On the lectern was the largest book I had ever seen. Standing behind the lectern was a "being." I say that because he had such a presence and power that was not human in nature.

He looked at me and announced in a rather loud authoritative voice, "Thy will has been done."

The book before him then opened, and I asked him what the book was. He told me it was the book of all the lives I had lived, ever! Now, that's one way of getting someone's attention, and I tried to see what was written on the pages but before I could get a really close look, he closed it with a satisfying snap! Isn't that always the way?!

Once again he announced, "Thy will has been done," but he said it more gently and with a kindly look on his powerful face.

I asked him what he meant by this and in a very matter of fact manner he said that I had accomplished all that I had wanted in this life, and now I had a choice to go back to spirit or stay on Earth and look at future options that were available to me.

In that instant that he said that, the knowledge came to me in a flash of intuition that I would stay and teach. As I said that to him, another insight came telling me if I had chosen to go back to spirit then I would have died of leukaemia. The being said all of this in a very authoritative manner.

"All is done," the being announced, and in that moment the room and the books and the lectern and the "being" all vanished, and I was in a very peaceful and wonderful state.

I stayed in this state for the rest of the meditation, and then we were brought back to conscious state. The usual format of these meditations was that we would all share what we has experienced, and as I sat there and listened to others there talking about visiting pretty gardens and talking to loved ones who had passed away, I thought how could I possibly follow what they had gone through without sounding melodramatic? It was profound to me, and as I shared with the group what I has seen and heard, the room went rather quiet as everyone digested what I was sharing with them. I finished what I had to say and no one said a thing until someone piped up that it was time to all have a nice cup of tea. I laugh at that now. It was such a typical New Zealand, English sort of thing to say. Right, well, that's all very interesting, and we are not actually sure what to say or how to respond, so let's all have a nice cup of tea, and we will all feel better!

I left the meeting that night feeling very different from what I had ever felt before. It was not just the physical feeling; I could sense that there had been some sort of inner shift. I had changed something. I had negotiated a new deal that would affect me for the rest of my life, and it felt very right and very peaceful.

That night I set myself on the road that took me closer to working with source energy and that night I became more aware of my God nature. After that, I felt the presence of spirit always with me, and I felt loved and protected. I felt I was being watched and monitored, guided and empowered. The feelings were stronger than ever before, and it wasn't seeing or hearing spirit. It was just simply there—this constant energy that was drawing me further away from my human nature and showing me my God nature.

Shortly after this meeting I had a dream that Kay and I were standing in a long line of people, and we were actually all waiting to be led through a door that led to the spirit realms. Actually, it wasn't a door; it was, in fact, a plastic multi-coloured fly screen that you see over the door at some people's houses over the summertime!

As we were waiting, a voice called out to us that we were ready, and that we could come through. I felt a bit like we were jumping the queue, but I suppose if you are ready then, well, you are ready, and I wasn't about to argue the point. So we went through the fly screen and began walking a path that was surrounded by countryside with mountains in the distance. I recall so vividly that all the surroundings seemed to be totally bleached of colour. The feeling was very neutral, and I recall watching people re-living karmic experiences, so that they could have more understanding of why they died and the ways they had lived their lives. I recall one man being shot over and over again until he understood something about his life, and when he did, he stopped being shot and moved on up the path!

We came to this big building that had pillars and huge rooms. As we went into the building, I started to fly, and I was buzzing around this huge room and bouncing off the walls. The feeling was heavenly. This went on for some time, and I was aware that Kay was in the background though I don't know what she was doing. The dream then finished, and I awoke with a huge smile on my face. After that I consistently had flying dreams all over the world and out into space. It was such a blast, I tell you!

As I progressed with my God nature, I carried on with my job and life, but with this added attachment of God that expanded my perception of everything. As I pursued this new dimension that I had added to my life, I had a constant feeling that what I was doing was leading somewhere. I think the same can be said for many of us who embark on such a profound journey. As our lives change because of the recognition of our god nature, we change everything about our vibrations and also affect the vibration of all around us and with us.

One thing I discovered was the importance of doing what you can and not to feel that by being God you have some huge obligation to everything and everyone. When some people get to this point, they may set up unrealistic goals for themselves and end up pressuring themselves with unattainable aims. I've seen people being very happy in life who make great changes that further enhance that happiness and then become unhappy because they created a belief system that what they were living was not good enough because as God, you had to be better.

It brings to mind what Tabaash says, "Enlightenment is living life with all the lights on."

Once we do see everything, then we must use our common sense and do what is possible without having to push the boat out too far. We are all good enough right now, and because we are all source energy, there will always be unlimited choices. Despite that fact, we also come with what I will call "Natural boundaries" that stop us from being distracted from our chosen path.

Focusing on being everything "ALL THE TIME" can itself be a major distraction. Once you have made the connection with God nature, then you have to go to your human plan and decide the best ways you can participate in life and turn your plans into feasible realities.

You might want to be a famous movie star or a great athlete, write a book, have a boat, etc., but it may never happen. And it's not happening because you can't do and be all these things but because your soul is saying that there are other things that you will succeed in better. We all come with certain traits that are our vocations, and we have to accept that our fantasies may not be these. It may simply be your vocation to be a good parent, have a normal job with a great day-to-day life that you are totally satisfied with and good friends and harmony, a loving family—well-being in every respect. And that really is good enough! As you develop, you remember what seems most natural to you, and you discover the things that you really excel at. As you do this, make sure you really indulge and make it your prime investment, mastering everything in ways that are totally appropriate for you.

For some, this does mean fame and fortune and life in the public eye. This does not mean that these people are an elite group, chosen to have luck on their side though. Those souls have chosen life to experience it in that way, allowing them to live out the way they chose to evolve through those circumstances. People often complain that why could they not have had that life and been rich and famous or whatever rather than pay attention to who they are and create new ways to evolve. Wishing to be someone else or live someone else's life is never ever going to take you to your authentic self. It will only keep you stuck in that old belief system until you turn the light on and really see yourself.

It is ok to be who you are now, and it's so central to your own personal advancement that you don't push yourself out of your comfort zone to such a degree that you find yourself in a place that takes you away from your core and makes you frightened and disheartened. As you master your life, there is no one more qualified to run it than you. Remember that wherever you find yourself, it is exactly where you *thought* yourself to be.

There is the saying that "death is a part of life," but I would change this and instead prefer to say, "Life is a part of death." Those who have embraced their God nature realize that there really is only life and living and that the idea of death does not even come into the equation. Death of the physical body only came about because human nature got so far away from source energy that the only way to once again be source energy was for the body to "die," so the soul could be free to be its authentic nature. The soul doesn't go anywhere and never has; it simply assimilates all that it is and focuses on what it may choose to experience. How can you go somewhere when you have never left?

Life being a part of death is pretty much the same. How can there really be death when there is only life, and that you never leave life, you simply leave your impression of what life was, and you move onto another one. Every day you are all creating new ways to live and through this, you are discovering how many aspects of energy make your personal life experience unique to you alone. It's so essential that you all get this to ensure that you create the best life you can physically, mentally and spiritually. It's never going to be who you have to become that will make the quintessential difference, but more who you *are*. And if who you are in your thoughts is taking you to a place that is going to make you *find* instead of *be*, then your journey will not be very palatable. Who you are all the time is, of course, everything, but where are you placing "this is who I am"? Imagine that you are going to sit in the sun and read your book, soak up the rays and generally have a relaxing time. You have all the beach paraphernalia that you need, and as you wander the beach, you are on the look-out for the best position.

Now, we have come to a fork in the road here, as there are choices. None of the choices will be wrong, but the choice you make will simply give you a different experience that will offer wisdom. Let's take the road to the left first. Ah, perfect place to settle, nice and sheltered and quite private but offering up a nice view of the beach and anything of interest that may get your attention. There is a nice bit of shade but lots of sunshine as well. It's flat so easy to put up the beach chair or roll out that towel and be comfortable. There is a lovely gentle breeze coming up from the beach which isn't too far away from the surf should you want to have a dip to cool off. Most would agree, perfect position, couldn't have done better myself—or is it?

Let's take the road to the right now. I've walked up and down and decided that I will set myself right on the shoreline. Sands a bit wet from the waves coming in, but once I've got the chair settled and I'm in, that will stabilize things. It's rather blowy and as the waves come in, it keeps taking all my things into the water, so I have this merry beach dance going on as I keep wading out to retrieve things. It's not that relaxing as I'm anxious about the next wave, and I can't read my book as the wind keeps flipping the pages. I'm tense, I'm not enjoying myself at all, and all my things are sopping wet, and there goes my book into the sea as the wind just whipped it out of my hands and carried it into the surf.

So Why Don't You Move?

Indeed? Why don't you move instead of stay in a place that does not make you happy?

The thing is whatever choice is made is simply a different experience. And that's why it's so vital to understand what sort of life experiences you want and to know that you don't need to set yourself up in an uncomfortable situation to learn what is more productive and what is not. Not moving on from counter-productive situations does not mean that you are on the wrong road. At times in life a soul will allow a certain amount of counter productivity because it feels that it is an essential part of its growth. Invariably you see that you no longer need to do that, and so you move away from that idea and change the energy. In other words, I've moved away from the shore where I was getting wet and moved to a place that was much better. I suppose at times on this planet you have to get wet before you can be dry! Seeing things in this way purely from the human nature probably doesn't make a great deal of sense, as most would wonder why anyone would want to be counterproductive.

Your higher nature though sees a great deal of sense in this as it's attuned to all the ways it can keep improving, and so it will lay out all the vantage points for growth.

There is no such thing as a limited experience—only a limited way of thinking about the experience.

As your thinking becomes clearer, then you "see" that you can position yourself in a more productive manner. Reminders are needed though—at times gentle and at times not so gentle. However they may come to you, they are established by you.

You are all setting yourselves up all the time.

It's unfortunate that too many on Earth are still setting themselves up from a point of conflict to be reminded. Conflict only comes about because you have reached a point where you can't be what you were, and your higher nature is in a conflict of interest with your human nature. Higher nature will keep pushing its point and will make human nature aware through discomfort of the need to change. Higher nature knows that conflict is not the natural state of affairs. It is a completely excessive and uncalled for way of having to change and is totally preventable.

Focus on life and living. Walk the beach and find the best place. Ensure you have all that is essential for a comfortable and pleasurable experience. It is your karma, yes, but your karma is only the deals that you have made and you can keep on making new ones all the time. There's always going to be another beach with a different view, and it will be easier to get a car park and find the place that you want to be without any form of conflict.

Do you like being swamped by the waves?

The unfortunate consequences of not choosing a better position on the beach, so to speak, is the physical implications it has on people. I am, of course, referring to physical health issues. Your body is created to sustain a great deal but the reality is, it does not recognize ill health. Physical health issues come about because of trapped energy that was ignored, and, therefore, the inevitability is that the energy turns into a physical disease because there is energy *dis-ease* in the system. One has to remember that everything about your whole being, physical or non-physical is the God energy. This energy can never go away, and this energy is always accessible to you in every way possible. What does rather *get in the way* though is the aspects of you that allow that idea of *dis-ease* to play a part in your life. And if this is happened to you or is happening to you, then have a look at where you have positioned yourself.

All of this, of course, is still the deal that you have made, and this deal fits in with all that you want to understand through that experience. If you have positioned yourself in such a way where you understand the deal and all that its means to you, then from that point you consider your options. And this is where I need to tell you that this is why some people will pass to spirit, and some will survive their illness to live a longer and fuller life. And this is *despite* the fact that you have connected to source energy, and know how to use it, etc., so what this is saying is that some souls will literally *choose the death of the physical* as their journey, and they are ok with that.

Why would anyone want to choose death?

It's not so much that they choose death but that the greater part of them knows when enough is enough, and it's time to move on. As I have mentioned, the soul only knows that there is life. So when the soul passes, it simply carries on living, and it lives without the confinement of the human emotions that will at times detain you. People get angry at death, and they get angry at illness, and they get angry that they can't control it or understand it or change it. Any negative response comes about because there is something that you are not connected to. And what you are not connected to is that there is always life. People are often afraid of death because they see it as the end of life and the leaving of everything they know and who they know, etc. If you were connected to the idea of life as ongoing, be it in physical or non-physical, then you would never feel these things.

Do you know that you will never ever feel sadness in spirit?

When people get sick, it is not because they have done something wrong. It is because a choice has been made allowing them to experience something in an extreme manner. This allows them to look at the position they are in life, and if they follow the indicators and make changes, they review their options and from there make a decision about *where in life they choose to be.*

CHAPTER TEN

Well, since I'm here, I might as well listen to myself.

Unknown

After this entire initial awakening, life began to be simply "life." Kay was recovering well from her cancer, and, in fact, we had pretty well forgotten that she had even been through such a thing. I felt though like I was rather treading water, feeling that there was a direction but not sure what way to go. I left the clothing shop and briefly went back into hospitality, working for one of the major hotel chains. I worked in the restaurant, then in reception, and then became a housekeeper. It just wasn't me, and, in fact, I had no idea what was. I felt like a bug hopping from bush to bush. I was now in my late twenties and felt rather unsettled and unsure. Yes, I may have had God on my side, but I had no sense that I was achieving anything or going anywhere. I thought I would have some time out. I had some savings and considered taking a month or two sabbatical from work in the hope I would get a sense of where I needed to be.

That idea lasted all of two weeks. I was in town one day and was passing a fur shop called English and Foreign Fur Company. Kay and I were familiar with the owner of the shop who was called Zena Slucki. She had come to New Zealand from Poland in the 1930s and had established her business that went on to flourish. Kay had bought a fur from her some time ago, and whenever I was in town, I would pop into the shop to say hello. And so that was my intention one afternoon, but the long and short of it was that Mrs. Slucki offered me a job, and I said no, but by the time I had walked home, I had this compelling feeling that I had to take the job, and so I rang her when I got home and accepted.

Why was I so compelled to accept this? It turned out that it was the last year of her life, and I ended up playing a major part in it. Mrs. Slucki was elegant and intelligent, a shrewd businesswoman. She was about 5'2" in her stockings and had a formidable air to her, and she was a born salesperson. Her husband had been a well-known doctor and had passed away in the 1950s. Even though I didn't know it at the time of starting work for her, I was there to look after her, and I will say it was a great honour and pleasure. There actually wasn't a lot to do as it was at the point where people were not wearing furs anymore, and yet every morning we went through the motions and maintained the "salon."

She had cancer, and as the illness progressed, she would spend more and more time at home though she always kept her finger on the business pulse. After all, it was her life, and even when she should not have been in the shop, she would come in and simply sit at her little French writing desk and hold fort. My chair was slightly behind there as if to make sure of the pecking order, but it gave me a good vantage point to keep an eye on her. I was terrified that she was going to die in the shop. One afternoon we had been chatting away, and after a while, she had gone silent—not unusual as she would often drop into a little nap. This went on for some time though, and I began to feel a bit anxious, and so I quietly went up to her and saw that her head was leaning on her chest. It was hard to see if she was breathing or not.

I bent down slightly closer but could not sense that she was breathing and so got a little bit closer. By this time my heart was pounding as I really thought that she had died. We were almost face-to-face, and at that moment she suddenly opened her eyes, and we both let out a yell of fright. Then she began to laugh, thank goodness, so I laughed back. We never said a thing, but I knew that she knew what I had been thinking.

A couple of days after that, we were just about to close for the day, and she had what I have since referred to as "a fur fit." For whatever reasons only know to herself, she suddenly started to pull all of the jackets and coats off the racks and throwing them onto the floor, the whole time muttering about how they were all in the wrong place and that I had no idea about how to display them properly. I looked on in dismay at the pile of furs. Having denuded all the racks of the furs, she then sat down and started to read a newspaper. She said nothing to me or didn't even look up. I simply started to hang everything back up, and in exactly the same way they had been before. It actually didn't take that long, but I was fuming and finding it hard to say nothing.

After everything had been replaced, she stood up looked at everything and then announced, "That's much better. Now we can go home"!

I began to wonder what our connection was and if we had ever know each other in a past life. There was ease between us and a sense of familiarity. That night I had a dream that made everything very clear to me. In the dream I was a young French woman, and I was the ladies maid to a wealthy older woman in France. That woman was Mrs. Slucki. In the dream there was to be a big grand party and as the ladies maid, I had laid out a selection of gowns for the mistress to choose.

Well, she got so angry with me and started throwing all these gowns at me and yelling and screaming. I walked out on her and never went back. Then in the dream I saw myself still as the young woman, and I was sitting on a beach that was all little stones.

A voice then said, "In that life you did not finish your karma with her. Now in this life as Blair she really needs you, and you must serve her in the best way."

The whole dream was in French, and I understood every word of it even though in this life my French is very, very minimal. After that dream I felt that I knew what I had to do, and I served her to the best of my ability. She stopped coming to the shop after a while, and I would go up to her place every Saturday after work and take her the mail and any other business she wanted to deal with.

One afternoon I arrived and was, of course, still dressed in my work clothes. I gave her all the mail, etc., and then asked if there was anything else she wanted me to do. She thought I had come to do her lawns, and when I told her no, she started to get very agitated, and so I had to mow her bloody lawns in my good shoes and trousers etc. I so laugh now when I think about it.

Having mowed the lawns, I went back into the house and she said, "She was going to have a little nap, and could I stay awhile?"

I sensed that what she really wanted was some company, even though she was going to sleep, so I agreed, and she went off to have her nap while I rang Kay and told her that I might be some time! After a couple of hours of watching television I thought that perhaps she would like to have something to eat. I started banging around in the kitchen making her an omelette and found a nice tray and a little vase for a flower and a nice napkin and nice silver cutlery and then walked up the hall to her bedroom to give her the omelette.

Well, she was certainly wide awake, the poor thing. She had completely forgotten that I was there and had obviously been terrified as she heard all the noise I was making in the kitchen. God knows what she was feeling what she heard the footsteps coming up the hall walking towards her bedroom. When she saw me, the relief was very evident!

"Oh it's you!"" she said with obvious relief. "I forgot that you we here."

Towards the end of the year she went into a private hospital where she died.

The shop closed in November of 1989, and Kay and I had decided that we would go the UK to visit some of her family that were there and make a trip to Egypt. Just before we went away, we went to a service at the Wellington Spiritualist Church. A well-known medium called Mary Fry was speaking and giving readings that night so we thought we'd go and see her. The evening was coming to a close, and she was about to sit down when suddenly she stood up again and came up to me.

She said, "I have this small lady here who has a foreign accent, and she is calling you son and wants to thank you for everything that you did for her."

What can I say? When she died, she had no children, and any family were offshore. To this day, I go to her grave and tidy it up and have a wee chat.

Kay and I went on our trip to the UK and Egypt and had a great experience. When we went to Egypt, I felt like I had gone home—such was the familiarity.

It was on a felucca down the Nile that Kay suddenly said to me "I think something has happened to my Mother."

For the last few years, Kay's mother, who had Alzheimer's, had been in a care home, and we had not seen her for some time.

On our return to the UK, Kay was told that her mother had passed away, and after a few calculations realized it was on the same day that Kay had the feeling in Egypt that something had happened. We both went to a spiritualist church meeting in Belgrave Square in London later that week, and there was a medium from Norfolk speaking. He came to Kay and gave her a very clear message from her mother, and it was wonderful.

Then he came to me and said, "That spirit wants to talk about your career choices."

"Now this is going to be interesting," I thought.

He told me he saw two rooms, and one had a big building in it with a red cross on it. I deduced that this was a hospital as once again I had been thinking about a medical career. Then he said another room was full of light, and whichever room I chose, I would excel in. I had no idea whatsoever the room full of light could be, and pretty well dismissed it, thinking I must be on the right track in regards to medicine.

We returned to New Zealand, and I felt very inspired to focus more on meditation and spiritual books. I felt like I was in some sort of transit zone. All the aspects that made up me seemed to be doing some sort of sorting of light dance, finding a place where everything would align itself. I went back to working in retail for the moment, and it was while I was at work one day that I had this odd feeling that spirit was telling me something. It was like this inner whisper that was heard by my soul, and though my human nature was unsure about what was being said, my soul knew exactly. This feeling stayed with me for many days, and it began to niggle at me a bit as I felt I was on the brink of something but had no inkling what.

Returning from work one afternoon I flicked on the television ready to watch the evening news. It wasn't quite news time yet and on the telly was a woman being interviewed, and she so happened to be a spiritual channel. As I watched the program, I had knew that what I had been feeling all week had something to do with channelling. I didn't know in what way, but I watched that program and by the end of it, I felt like I had to try this and see how it worked for me.

I had no clue what to do, so I just went with what I felt. I mentioned all this to Kay, and she was open to exploring so having no idea what to expect or do, we lit a candle, dimmed the lights, and sat across from each other at the table linking hands. To be perfectly honest, I felt a bit silly, and it all seemed a bit too New Age for my liking. We breathed deeply and giggled a bit, and then started to settle down.

It was very quiet in the room, and I started to feel very still and peaceful and just went with that feeling. I wasn't aware of time at all. It was a moment, and we were in it, and I was going to let whatever happens, happen. At some point a great deal of energy coursed through my body, and I recognized this as a link to spirit. Then a deep almost overwhelming feeling of sadness came upon me that seemed to have nothing to do with me but then seemed to have everything to do with me and everything and everybody else as well.

At the time I couldn't really define it properly, but now all these years later, I can see that I was tuning into the collective sadness of all consciousness on this planet, and I felt the tears running down my face as if I was quietly mourning for something that we had all lost. I was also being washed with an energy of everything that was good, and then I felt words come into my mind that were not from me. It was a voice in my head, but it was not a voice like someone talking but more like the idea of the voice and the emotions and personality of someone. I felt like I had to literally speak what I was getting in my mind and so I just opened my mouth to let the words flow.

I had made a connection with Kay's Father, who had passed away about a year before, and he was talking to me, and I was relaying what he was saying to Kay.

I was very conscious of what I was saying but also felt detached as if I was the observer as much as the participant. Certain facts seemed to ring very true to Kay and then as quickly as it happened, it then finished, and I could feel the withdrawal of its energy. I found myself feeling quiet and still and filled with an energy that was both peaceful as much as it was stimulating.

When I eventually opened my eyes, Kay was sitting before me, looking amazed and at the same time a bit perplexed about what had happened. Interestingly for me, I felt very matter of fact and that what had happened was very natural. I stood up and turned the light on and had to walk around for a while. Kay I and didn't say anything to each other. This did not seem the time for words. We all have things that happen to us in our lives, and when they do, we know that we can never go back to how things were before. We make a new agreement when these things happen, and this agreement will always herald in more changes, more growth, and more challenges in many ways.

What started for me then was to totally thrust myself in all ways that I never thought possible, and at times I did not like what I saw and felt and experienced. I wasn't against anything, but I began to really grasp the true meaning of self-development and understood it to be the total development of my life on all levels. I saw more clearly that in each life we live we have to see who we are in every way and be completely accountable for our actions and thoughts, attitudes, etc. I was facing myself completely, and at times what I saw I didn't like or want to accept. It was blunt and raw and honest and painful as I also looked back and saw how I could have done things differently to avoid some of the unhappy events in my life. And as I grew from this and made changes, I grew up and evolved in every way possible.

Kay and I started to have nightly meditation/channelling sessions to see what would happen. I expected more messages to come through like before, but instead I would sit there and my body would be filled with so much energy that it was almost painful. Often my arms would levitate, and for an hour I could sit in deep peace holding up my arms without any discomfort. As time progressed, my legs started to do the same thing, and I must have looked a comical sight with my bum firmly planted on the ground while my arms and legs were suspended! Other times I would be shaking like I was having some sort of fit as the energy would course through my system. This would also make me feel a bit nauseous at times though I never had the feeling to be sick. As these things happened, the idea came to me that the body was adjusting itself to working with a vibration that was higher than my body normally experienced. I felt that I was being guided and monitored through this whole process. Never did I feel concerned and always had a feeling that I was in good hands throughout this whole process.

After a while, my apprenticeship as a contortionist seemed to abate, and then the energy then moved up and into my vocal chords. I would sit there in our "practices" feeling great joy and peace, but all these weird sounds were emitting from me. Deep moans and grunts, vowel sounds in all pitches, the neighbours must have thought that I was completely deranged or having some really great sex! Nevertheless, I persevered and allowed whatever was happening to happen.

It felt right all the time, and as time went by I could feel the positive changes being made to me. I was more energized and focused. I could feel a new sense of being and determination arise in me. I really was experiencing that *something more* on a greater physical level. It was very present, and I had no sense of where it was going.

There are just some things that you just know are *right* to do, and this was one of them for me. I felt like I was being trained for something, and I also felt like I was stepping further away from the idea of myself, and seeing myself more through my soul. It was at times a very odd feeling, as I knew it was my body, but when I looked at myself in a mirror, what was looking back at me wasn't my physical self. At times that made me fearful and anxious as I felt I was exposing something of myself that I could not ever hide again. I knew that what I was developing was stripping away every layer of resistance and ignorance. It was showing me the games I was playing and making me aware on every level that what I was, I had created, and what I was creating was always the platform for more of me and more of the life that would come with what I was all about. It was very disconcerting, as there was really nowhere to hide.

And that's what we do—we all hide from what we are and create these illusions that give us a false sense of how we identify with our life. In those illusions are a whole lot of rules and rituals that only serve to confuse us more and bury us deeper in our fears and distractions. Anyone who has gone through all of this—and I know there are many—would know that as much as it is pleasant to gaze upon our authentic self, it also can be an exceedingly scratchy experience as you gain knowledge of all of you. The more we are God; the deeper we go into knowing self.

I see now that going through all of this truly exposes the aspects of self that need to be changed. It is not so much that they are wrong, but more that they are counterproductive to us, and if you can look honestly at them, you can change the way they affect you. Always being someone who would get in the head too much and prone to fear and self-effacement, I took what I was seeing hard and made things so much harder for myself. After a while I could see that I had to turn my self-effacement into confidence and my fear into having more faith in my power. I had to eliminate those old ideas of myself, and to this very day, I am still doing that. Being God doesn't mean that you stop everything; you just know how to manage it much better.

My body began to feel more settled during the meditations, and I could greatly sense the presence of spirit with me. As time progressed, I started to connect with spirits who had passed over, but for some reason they were a bit locked into a holding pattern before they could truly go to God. It seemed that it was our task to assist these souls to do this, and I would receive information from source energy to give to these souls, and at times Kay would talk to them and help them understand that they were able to release themselves from whatever was holding them.

We did this for some months, and there was one soul whose name was Paul. He was French, and he had died in the 1960s. He told me that he had been in some secret service, had been kidnapped, tortured and then died. We worked with him several times, and then one evening I was chatting to him in my thoughts and this enormous light exploded in my head, and I could see his soul flying towards this light, and then the light closed. It was quite a profound experience for me as it was so very real in every way possible. Seeing that light brought out a deep yearning in me that I had for days afterwards. This was not the last I was to see of Paul though.

Life with spirit was very real to us now on a daily basis and living in such a way made life more real and amplified. I looked forward so much to having our evening catch-up with spirit but also felt like I had somehow plateaued and was ready for more. More came a few weeks later when I was sitting peacefully waiting for "something" to happen when the unmistakable energy of Paul presented itself to me. I was surprised but very pleased, and he said that he had been assigned to me to "work off some karma" by assisting me in my development as a channel. I was curious about what karma he was working off but never pushed the point! All other souls seemed to have stepped aside, and Paul became the main event. As the weeks passed, he would present himself to me in my thoughts and encourage me to "channel" him. In those days I was a conscious channel and was 100% aware of all that was said. Paul would come through and present basic teachings, or he would simply chat away to Kay and, of course, to me in my head! It really was like developing a friendship, getting to know each other and share and hang out in an odd sort of way. Paul did this for about a year, and I became very accustomed to him being there, not just channelling him but the feeling of his presence as a normal part of my life.

Then one evening Paul came through and announced that this was the last time he was going to be with us as it was time for him to move on in his development and also for him to make way for someone else. I was really upset as it was truly like saying goodbye to someone that you loved dearly. He had become a part of us, and I would miss him greatly. He didn't hang around at all that evening. He just came to tell us what was happening, and then with his farewell, he simply departed. That's the thing I have learned about working with spirit. They deal with the facts of things, and once it's time to move on, they do.

It wasn't long before I started to feel the presence of another energy and the interesting thing about this one was that it felt like I was connecting with someone that I had known. A big smiley face appeared in my mind one evening when I was having a meditation, and he told me his name was Astania.

Then he took me on a little journey—well maybe not so little, as it was profound to me. He took me to a life that we had together in Egypt when he was my father, and I was his son. It truly felt like a reunion, and I was overcome from the emotion of the connection. It was quite an extraordinary experience, and everything about it made sense, and I felt the energy of that life and who I was with him as his son. And so we settled into a new pattern of learning, as Astania presented some quite profound teachings. Other friends who were on their own spiritual journeys began to come and sit with us, and Astania would talk and they could ask questions. All the practice was good for me and, of course, was allowing my body to become even more used to the energy of spirit. Astania's energy was different from Paul's. It vibrated at a higher frequency, and so there were some adjustments that had to be made. It always felt good, and I always felt good and right about what was happening. I never thought of it as channelling dead people but just bringing through consciousness on that level. It seemed to fit in with what was natural to me.

I was making progress as a channel and progress as a person, but I really had no idea where any of this was taking me. It certainly was making a huge difference in my life as it helped me to develop as a person and understand the supposed bigger picture of life. Kay had all but recovered from her cancer, and we were really settled in our lives on all levels. After some months I began to really feel the energy of what I could only describe as a big presence. I felt that it had locked into my grid, and that it seemed to want to stay. I also felt that I was being observed and that whatever it was, needed me to know that it was there, and I felt like I was being prepared for something.

This feeling never left me, and I got so used to it that it became a part of my consciousness to such a degree that I almost forgot that it was there. I seemed to fit into it as much as it was fitting into me. After a while I never gave it a thought and just got on with everything. One afternoon I was skimming through the paper and at the back there was a small advertisement for a meeting that night of a spiritual channel. It was a woman who channelled the Egyptian goddess Isis. A green light was flashing in my mind in such a way that could not be ignored; I knew that Kay and I had to attend that meeting. And so we went.

There were a lot of people in the room wanting to hear the teachings of Isis. I had not seen a channel work before and so was interested to compare how it was with the way I was doing it. Isis came through a woman called Jenny and when she did she used the body as if it were her own. She used the eyes and was very animated in the body. There were noticeable differences that made it evident that "Jenny" had stepped aside. Isis spoke in a clear and distinct way, presenting her teachings to the audience. At one point she suddenly stopped and stared into the crowd. She then pointed out into the crowd and said, "You are a channel." I never assumed for a moment that she was talking about me; I thought she was referring to someone behind me. Then I realized that everyone was staring at me and, of course, then I became very self-conscious and could feel a deep blush creep up into my face. She said some other things that I can't remember but that meeting was to be a turning point for my life.

Jenny "Isis" ran weekend workshops, and Kay and I signed up for one of them and what a wonderful experience it was. There were about thirty in the group, and many of us created a great bond that lasted for years and years. I loved it all and felt so at ease and comfortable about what we were learning. My whole being seemed to reach for what was being offered and accept it with such alacrity. We did several of these Isis workshops, and every time we grew and expanded in whom we were as Gods and as men and women on a soul journey. My energy must have been accelerating because of this as the presence that had been around seemed to get stronger, and one day a face appeared in my mind's eye of a man with strong features, a big wide smile and eyes that told a lot of stories. That was the first time I had a vision of Tabaash. There were no words, just this powerful man looking at me with great presence and great love. It was very humbling, and I don't mind saying very overwhelming as well. Who was this character and what did he want with me?

We became friends with Jenny and her husband, and they would come to our house when they were in Wellington and use one of our rooms as a place where Isis could do private consultations for people. It was during one of those visits that Isis was talking to me, and she told me that that there was the presence of Tabaash around me, and that he wanted to work with me. What she said just made so much sense to me, and I felt that now I had an answer. Now I had some direction in regards to who I was and what I needed to do. Once that became clear to me, I literally invited in Tabaash, I started to speak to him and ask for his guidance and what he needed me to do. I was still bringing in Astania but could feel that Tabaash and his energy was getting bigger and bigger.

I meditated more and followed what my feelings were saying. I upped my workouts at the gym feeling the need to be stronger and fitter. I altered my diet. I felt I was re-creating myself for something that I had chosen but to get there, I had to put the work into it. On a winter's evening as we were doing the usual evening meditation, Tabaash pulled the cork and presented himself with no big build-up or announcement. He simply arrived instead of Astania.

God, I'm sitting here now all these years later writing about this and suddenly feeling quite emotional. And also I'm wondering had he presented me with the story over the next twenty-five years, would I have gone down that track. I don't know what to say to that except it's been the most challenging time of my life in every way possible. Regardless of the service to others, it's been my growing up, it's been me facing myself, and it's been me having to be accountable for me and my actions and attitudes—my whole life. By agreeing to be the channel for Tabaash, I was setting myself up in front of myself all the time in such an amplified way that I could never ignore it. Did I ever doubt what I was doing? Yes. Did I ever want to stop doing it? Yes. Did I ever question my sanity? No, and I never thought for a moment that I was mad. I recall one woman who was a nurse asking me how I knew I wasn't suffering from multiple personality disorder.

I said, "Well, if I am, it seems to be doing a bloody good job."

I hated the way people would look at me when I told them my job was a channel. They looked at me like I was some sort of freak. Being a channel has given me a lot but it also has divided me and separated me from a lot as well, and I would not change a thing.

Right from the beginning of my life, I seemed to single myself out as someone who had to step out on that limb, so to speak, and reach for something that would make a difference. I had to be raw and exposed in a sense; I had to stand-alone and not be or have what other people would have in their lives. I can see now it's about service and this is simply that way that I have chosen to do it. From the moment Tabaash came through it changed everything and offered up a whole new cornucopia of life's experience's that made me stand up and face my fears.

TABAASH SPEAKS

People often speak of their destiny as if they have had no other choices in the life they are living. A destiny is a commitment that you have forged before you were born. It is something that is essential to your development, and often as is the case, the development of others individually and on a mass scale. It will fit into your everyday life and, of course, change your everyday life. Destiny does not "single" you out. It is simply the choice you have made to evolve.

Collective consciousness works in an interesting way here. Some souls will choose to participate in a destiny that involves many other souls. They will choose to be a part of a certain event that has major implications on their own karma as much as it would of the people they are connected with and, in some cases, the world. In recent times the events of 9/11 are a prime example of such a situation. All those souls who departed into spirit that day had basically signed up for the event, consequently expanding their own consciousness by participating in being victims of an act of terrorism. The ripple effect their participation had will influence millions of people throughout history for many centuries to come. And all those souls who departed that day knew that and wanted it to be a part of their own personal experience in life. The same can be said for any soul who has chosen to be a part of conflict on a mass level. The great wars of the 20th century are also a prime example of souls who choose to be a part of a major drama on Earth.

This is a time to remind you that every conscious and unconscious moment of your life you are emitting energy. It is all your thoughts and words and deeds—all interpreted as vibration—and this becomes your life. This is the same for everybody, and if you have a collective thought, be it consciously or unconsciously, this has a collective impact on the world and the events that will happen. For example, imagine a performer on the stage having just presented a performance, and now imagine the audience applauding loudly standing and shouting with praise and adoration for the performer. Imagine flowers being thrown upon the stage. The vibration of that not only is sent to the performer, but it is also infectious to the audience, and the roars and cheers get louder and louder as they vibration is "caught" by everyone. Now imagine the total opposite: the audience is not clapping at all and throwing verbal insults to the performer. There is much derision and booing, and this energy also is infectious and at some point a mass chant of "OFF, OFF, OFF, OFF" fills the theatre. One can imagine how the performer would feel.

This happens in the world as well in every way possible, and you are all a part of what is being created. At times it is hard to stand up in the face of adversity as many have found out. I think of people who have been conscientious objectors through the wars on this planet and how they have been branded as cowards.

Since your destiny is your commitment to your life and the choices that you have made for this life, you will naturally choose the physical, emotional and mental environments that offer up the best stage to play these out on. Poverty and war, terrorism, disease, economic recession, bigotry and racism, to name a few things, are some of those stages. They do not create themselves. It's out of the question that those examples would ever have a life of their own. The same can be said of bad marriages and child abuse, being un-fulfilled at work and yes, ill health. It may sound a brutal way of putting it, but these things are literally commitments to life. People do make these things their destiny. They do this because these platforms offer up a plethora of experiences that will allow the soul to evolve them. Life is simply everything, and you will choose through your incarnations to literally experience everything. You will, of course, create platforms that will offer up joy and fulfilment, abundance and harmony as well, and you will learn much from that as you will from the opposite.

Often a question asked of me is "What am I here to do?"

I would always first answer that you are here to live as God and by living as God, you find the best platform to find to express the deals that you brought with you when you were born. I have made a list of ideas that you may wish to affirm through your days. Use them at your will. Use them often and remember that they carry a vibration that you are sending out to call back in.

I AM HERE TO LIVE MY LIFE.

I KNOW WHO I AM AND WHAT IS AUTHENTIC TO ME.

I ALWAYS HAVE TOTAL AUTHORITY OVER MY LIFE.

WHATEVER PLATFORM I LIVE FROM, I ACCEPT THIS WITH PEACE.

I CANNOT AND WILL NOT EVER MAKE MISTAKES.

I ACCEPT SOURCE POWER AS MYSELF.

MY SUCCESS IS EXPERIENCED DAILY. IT IS NEVER HOPEFULLY FOUND.

ONLY I CAN MAKE MY LIFE, AND I CHOOSE A GOOD LIFE.

I AM ALWAYS GOOD ENOUGH FOR BEING GOOD ENOUGH.

Simple examples, indeed, of how one can take a thought, turn it into a vibration, and then live it to make it work for you. Every time you affirm something, you will always get an answer back in some shape or form. If for instance you affirm "I AM HERE TO LIVE MY LIFE," then ideas will often pop into your mind as the best way that you can do this, or you may get a strong feeling about something you need to do. There is always silent dialogue that goes with everything, I like to call it *positive chatter*, and it's never intrusive. It's always going to be beneficial, and it will never stop! Affirming something is not enough; you must listen to that positive chatter that comes after you affirm, as that is an important form of guidance for you. You might affirm *I AM GOD* a thousand times in a day, but you still have to find ways of taking that affirmation and weaving it into your life and feel it and then live what you are feeling. The more you affirm, the more you recognize what your destiny (choices and commitments) is.

You are all playing out so many roles every day you live, and it's impossible to isolate any one of those roles as you. Human nature will limit themselves so much by trying to segregate one specific thing as who they are, what they are meant to be, do, etc. Is it not more infinitely stimulating to believe that you are everything and that you have a whole lifetime of expression and adventure? Before you all daily is the great adventure of life that needs expression in all the voices that you have. It is interesting to note that some synonyms for *destined* are *designed, intended* and *ordained.* So you see, you are designed for life, intended to live, and ordained to a destiny of infinite greatness; therefore, always access life in the all its power.

Try, as you all will at points in your life, to victimize your own personal existence, the inevitable is that you will succeed. It is as they say *"written in the stars,"* for all things that are aligned with God will bring about a life of balance. Be absolute in your in your efforts to find the voices that you can speak in your life. As these voices are presented to you, what may occur is that you will also be presented with the barricades that deny you of these voices. These barricades are never permanent, for nothing can lock you in since you always have the key to anything that may incarcerate you. The louder you make the positive voices, the less the barricades will be there, for how can they strengthen themselves against the force of your alignment with the power of all life?

It has always been and always will be your intention to do the best in each life. Your best though may be brought out in your sufferings or the sufferings of others as you are stimulated to look deeper into your soul through adversity.

Once the adversity is no longer there, you wish then to linger in your light and allow self to see what the light shows you. Such a time in history that you now live in has a particular vibration that you all were attracted to, and attracted to for its rawness and its undeniable brutal exposure of human nature. There is no simplicity in some of the rules that have been created by human beings. What is being said when a youth who should be indulging in the pleasures of life and growing would go into a school and gun down his fellows? What is the message to the masses when a government has no qualms about creating weapons of mass destruction and ignoring the plight of its own people and the plight of all peoples for that matter?

It is not ignorance, as it takes conscious high intelligence to support such ideas and a high level of awareness to know how to create a system that feeds conflict but starves peace.

There is always hope, for hope is higher than hate and the more that people hold onto and propagate the hope that is there, then the hate becomes like a disease that invariably destroys itself. For hate cannot and will not find an appetite for hope. The hate will then turn upon itself for there is nothing else to eat, and in its ego it will not even recognize that it is destroying itself before it is too late, and hope will then prevail.

Having chosen to live in a time of such extremities will, of course, place you in a situation where you can experience your "destiny" in extreme ways. Excessive pathways will make you more acute in your responses, be they positive or negative. This acuteness creates an intensity of interest from the higher part of you to explore the fields of learning that you have opened up. It's this very field of consciousness that is so exciting to the higher nature as it understands the energy is to be used to *resolve, connect, and create*. There have always been significant times in history on Earth where the option to evolve through extremes has been presented to human nature, and not just from experiences of conflict. Evolution of the soul, of course, has occurred through artistic endeavours and scientific discoveries. Many souls through history have used these times to bring about positive changes that have benefited all mankind. These events are occurring all the time, particularly in this day and age with the technological advances that are consistently being made.

This is, of course, causes a great deal of interest to science as it advances in its technological pursuits. Perhaps they would not be so keen on being told that what they are really doing is advancing their understanding of vibration and, therefore, the energy of God! It has never ceased to amaze me that men and women of such high intellect can be so challenged by the hypothesis of God as a real energy. Perhaps it is the fear that there is something greater than thinking? Or perhaps it is more that the idea of such a thing touches them in places that they have secreted away their own authenticity. To bring to the fore such authenticity for some seems to be a thing of great danger. It touches the emotional and feeling parts of themselves, parts, which, of course, expose them to seeing and knowing in ways that thinking can never do.

However, it is still the choice of those souls to allow such a destiny, and they must live out what they must to the best of their abilities. Unfortunately, it is such choices that so often affect humankind in calamitous ways, but one must still accept that it's the will of all beings to be involved in life on whatever scale it may be.

You are all playing out what you have scripted through your thoughts, feelings and actions. It is not so much to stop the argument that you may be having with life and those and that which you are involved with, but more so the arguments that you may be having with so many of the selves that make you up. These arguments are the chatter that is petty and useless that is teeming within the minds of human beings. Often you may have heard or read about the significance of being *still in your mind,* and this need is not exaggerated as it is to the utmost benefit to all who may practice this. Stilling the mind is not as many assume stopping your thinking but more to control what thoughts assail you and have only those that bring you *peace of mind.* Regular practice of this allows you to be conscious of the waves of energy that you are receiving and subsequently allows you to be an observer of these thoughts before they become something unreliable or uncontrollable. On the following page is an exercise that will assist the stilling of the mind.

Stilling of the Mind Exercise

To still the mind is a much greater feat than to practice to still the body. The body will easily follow how the mind guides it. The mind itself will not pay heed to the body, as the mind knows that the body is not very mindful.

The practice of stilling the mind is not an arduous task that one must set for oneself. It is not some ruthless discipline that pains you in its discipline rather than gives you the joy of practicing it. I feel that stilling the mind is a practice that permits you to deeply listen, allowing the soul to hear the sound of life in all its grandeur. Stilling the human mind gives you the prospect of thinking as God would, therefore, eliminating the human chatter that so pervades most of human nature. Remove this chatter, and it is extraordinary what you will hear, as you will hear what all of your higher nature is speaking. This is not a cacophony of sound but more a feeling of everything that makes sense on the deepest level, knowledge beyond your human nature.

Read through this exercise and then consider recording it so you can listen to it as you move through this experience.

Sit in a place where you know you will not be disrupted.

If you wish, you may lie down with your hands by your sides. Do not cross your legs. If you choose to sit instead, place your feet firmly on the ground and rest your hands comfortably in your lap.

Breathe normally and let your body relax and find its own peaceful rhythm. If you have to scratch your nose, do so; if you have to cough, by all means cough! Resettle your body as you feel yourself beginning to relax.

Once you feel settled, be aware of your surroundings—the sounds you may hear, the feeling of the chair or the floor or the mat, etc. Allow all of this to simply be a part of you.

Focus for a moment on your breath. It should be easy and not too deep. As the body relaxes more, it will find its own natural breathing rhythm. Allow this to happen.

Focus on your heart chakra and imagine that as you breathe, you are literally expanding the idea of you beyond your body. Imagine that you have the idea that you the soul are standing before the body watching it as it goes through this process.

Once you feel you have accomplished this, create the idea that you are now expanding yourself beyond the room that you are in and see yourself floating above it.

Create the idea of what you are seeing and put your full attention on going up beyond it into a place where you feel that you are able to see the very city or place you live.

Allow the body to be more relaxed and now focus your attention on expanding yourself beyond Earth and see yourself looking down on Earth, floating like a green blue gem in space.

Let us go further out into deep space. When you feel you are there, just be still.

In deep space it is still and quiet, and you can feel your own stillness pervade. Allow your body now to know the benefits of this elixir of silence. Let it embrace you.

Your whole being is participating in this now. You are expanded beyond your human nature and allowing the human mind to think of God, and as God always thinks from a point of peace, then so do you. Create the idea that you accept this and keep repeating that four or five times, more of you wish.

Feel your body totally accept the stillness of the mind and allow the cells of the body to absorb the benefits of this.

Stay in this place as long as you wish. Trust that you will feel when it is appropriate to return to Earth, to your room, to your body.

Once you are "back to Earth," just allow yourself to sit quietly for a moment as you once again adjust to your human nature. Gradually let full awareness embrace you, and when you wish get up and have a glass of water.

Not only is this simple exercise taking you into a deep place where you can still the mind, it is also training your mind to develop visualization abilities and stronger directive aptitude. Expanding your attention beyond your physical reality is also reminding you that you are not just the physical body but an unlimited source of energy existing everywhere and a place that you can visit freely of your own will.

This time in your life is a time to create and hold onto a new vision of who you are and what you want to be more of. The impact of this will not only have a positive effect on you but on everyone and everything. Choosing the way you live is essentially choosing the way that everyone will live now and in the future. And I am not talking about what type of wall paper to use in the living room!

You are all presenting before you the blueprint of your personal futures and the future of planet Earth. It's an intimidating prospect creating life, and knowing that all of you intrinsically hold the future in your own hands. It is not the hands though that carry the future, but your own souls who will direct the force of life so that the human in you can construct creation with meticulous thoroughness.

It is very tiring being a human being with all its rules and rituals, its challenges and pressures. Why then not give up the idea of being a human being and instead embrace the idea of living as a *GOD BEING* with all the power leading the human being in such a way as to allow it to live its utmost potential?

Imagine all human beings worldwide standing still for a moment and raising their arms up to draw in source power. That source power is like fine lines of light that link with the bodies and ripple through healing and empowering. The mind bodies and the emotional bodies are doing the same, all reaching to God and drawing this energy in. All the "bodies" of energy that you represent align to "all beings," and in this alignment you feel a mass dance of collective consciousness being played out. This mass energy that is being created lifts all energy to a higher level and invites in more source power. The lines of light are multi-coloured, and as all beings blend more and more, this energy pervades all, and it expresses itself out into space surrounding all the dwelling places on this planet. All people and all things are touched by this energy and benefit from it.

This is what is happening now to you and all; this is what you are involved in at this point in your life. As each of you takes the steps to reach up for something higher and allows yourself to live this energy, and then all of you have the greatest of revelations, your own true authentic beings. So I say to you all, reach as high as you can and once you touch what is authentic, know that it will change your whole being in the very best way. Keep reaching every day of your life and in some way God, source power, higher nature, all that is, will meet you and hold on tight.

CHAPTER ELEVEN

One can never truly see something as real, as one will always find other ways to see.

Unknown

Once Tabaash presented his calling card, so to speak, everything changed in ways that were to demand of me so much more in every way possible. Astania simply vanished, stepping aside for Tabaash. I have noticed that disembodied energies have no sentimentality in regards to the work that they have to do. I am not saying they don't have love and compassion, but I have always had the feeling that they are here to do a job, and one must simply get on with it! No time for welcoming parties and farewell parties. Here's the fact, here I am, and this is what you need to do.

As I started to develop the ability to channel Tabaash I felt like we were part of a business team that had been put together, and the roles that we were playing were, simply put, the roles that we were playing. I had agreed to the role that I was playing before I was born; I had evolved my human life to the point where now it was time to live out that agreement. It all seemed very practical and uncomplicated. Any complications were always made by me in my fears and resistance to all that I was having to do and change, and I had to constantly remind myself that I was *NOT* being told what to do but fulfilling the agreement that I had made with my own higher nature.

My body was more used to working with the energy of spirit and so all that shaking and gyrating had long ago stopped. I felt compelled to get fitter and be more conscious of what I was eating. I had the sense of losing myself but also gaining more of me, and I must admit I did not like the feeling. It was like I was in a constant battle with some of those selves that did not want to let go. I felt worried that I was not doing it right and that I was going to let the higher "team" down. I was living my life, holding down a job, having a relationship, and through it all, taking down all of myself and exposing my soul, and I'm still doing it. This process does not stop.

One afternoon I felt compelled to have a meditation, so I went upstairs to the room where I now work and "plugged in" to God. I went in to a rather blissful space that was extremely euphoric and at some point Tabaash's face appeared in my mind's eye. He was looking at me with a big grin on his face, and he told me to open my eyes. I initially resisted this request as I was feeling so wonderful and didn't want to break that feeling. He repeated his request, and so I finally relented and opened my eyes. I wasn't in the room upstairs anymore. I was sitting on a floor of black and white marble tiles and to the right of me were large open windows with filmy curtains gently blowing into the room. There was a gentle and peaceful light that was outside. I looked up and saw Tabaash, standing in front of me laughing.

He said, "What are you sitting on the floor for, Blair?"

I gave no reply as I was pretty dumbfounded about what had happened and was trying to understand and get my bearings. I felt no fear at all. Tabaash reached down to me and took my hand and pulled me up.

"Come, come," he said. "Let's sit down and talk."

I stood up and followed Tabaash out of the room and went to the right where we sat down on what I shall describe as a squishy comfortable sofa that was a dark camel colour. Tabaash sat before me and started to talk to me of the agreement that as souls we had made to work together. He outlined the plan that we had made and the roles that each of us was to play. He spoke also of others who were a part of this plan that would step in and out through the years. He spoke of the teaching and the people that we would meet, and when we did, he said that all of us were triggers for our development as individuals as much as catalysts for growth on a mass level. He said that we were part of a greater team of "teachers and healers" who had agreed to participate in raising consciousness on Earth. He was very matter of fact, and it really was like he was presenting facts to me—facts that deep within I knew.

As he talked to me, I listened but also looked around at my surroundings. We seemed to be on an open balcony on the second level of a large house. There was a courtyard below, and on the level we were on I could see many other doors. It was a complete square, and as the years progressed with my work, I came to this place all the time—sometimes going into rooms where I would meet up with a teacher or guide. But at this point that was all still to come, and Tabaash must have felt that he had said enough for the moment as he told me it was time to return.

My eyes closed and once again I had the feeling of euphoria. In an instant I opened my eyes, and I was back in the room at home where I had started my meditation. I sat there for ages allowing what I had experienced to sink in. I felt very calm and matter of fact, and I relayed to Kay what had happened and what I had been told that we needed to do. And that was to keep practicing channelling Tabaash, which I fervently did every night. There was no "time" that Tabaash had mentioned when we might take the plunge and go public with what we were doing. I was somewhat ambivalent, I must admit, as I didn't want to set myself up to be ridiculed and thought crazy. Yes, it all made sense—what was happening—and yes, it was real, not something that I was making up, but even so, it was a huge plunge to take and yet plunge I did.

During the evening sessions with Tabaash, he would come through for an hour and just chat away to Kay, allowing her to ask questions and just generally chat really. It was very practical, and there was no big deal about it. In those early times my eyes were closed, and I was still conscious of what Tabaash was saying and the conversations he was having with Kay. In the winter they would sit in front of the open fire, Tabaash attending to it, with my eyes closed and never once did he set the house on fire. He said he just looked through my eyelids. Kay got used to this, and as she was chatting away to Tabaash would often be doing something like filing her nails. She was doing this one night and not looking at Tabaash but engrossed in what she was doing. Tabaash had been telling her that the time was coming soon that we would go public "with the work," as he called it, and that there were practical things to attend to. He had been poking away in the fire while he was doing this, and then he suddenly turned to Kay. I had left my body. Tabaash had opened my eyes and for the first time he was looking at Kay who was looking at Tabaash looking through me. That first experience for her of him using my eyes was quite a shock after spending so many months having conversations with him with my eyes closed.

Things progressed rapidly after that as Tabaash became more animated in my body, and he announced one day that it was time to hire a venue and present our very first public meeting. I can't begin to tell you how much fear that brought up in me. What was I doing, and why was I putting myself in such a situation? Why hadn't I just followed a normal career path and had a normal life like so many other people? Then I thought, "Well, maybe this is normal for someone like me!"

That first meeting is all a bit of a blur now. I had placed a very small add in the paper thinking that maybe we would get about 20 people, and when about 100 people showed up, that really set the fear flames burning. I remember walking down the aisle to the front of the room feeling silly and nervous, I had no idea at all what Tabaash was going to say and when he did would it be of any worth and would it be well received. I had been taught a method by spirit to leave my body and let Tabaash through, so I quickly departed and let Mr. T. do his thing. I think the meeting was about an hour and afterwards most of the hundred stayed behind to talk and to thank me for the meeting. Always a good sign, I'm not sure what I would have done if everyone had quickly left!

From that very first meeting we began to establish our profile, creating teaching evenings that we ran in the upstairs living area. We could sit about fourteen people around the room; Tabaash would present his teachings and often take the group through a guided meditation. Afterwards we would all have a cup of tea and something that Kay had baked for the group. I think people were just as keen on coming to see what Kay would bake for that evening—her orange muffins were a great hit!

I was approached by the Wellington Spiritualist Church to see if we would be the evening's guest "medium" at some of their Sunday services. Tabaash was really keen on participating in as much as possible to get me more used to the public profile and, of course, to present his teachings. I've always been a rather shy person though I'm sure some would disagree. Taking such a step was really hard for me, but I learned a lot in those days about talking to people and presenting myself. As word got round, we eventually did the rounds of most of the Spiritual Churches in the Wellington region and were even asked to be their guest speaker at their national conference. We created a radio program on community Access Radio called "Talking with Tabaash" where Tabaash would do a teaching and then open the phone lines so that people could ring up and ask questions. After a while we changed the format where Tabaash would do his teaching and then he would interview an invited guest. I knew quite an array of people, so we had some interesting guests on that show over the two years we did it.

After the show we would always take our guest out to a place called Strawberry Fare that was a desert restaurant. The place used to be an old funeral parlour started in the 1800s—to me, that seemed very appropriate! So over plates laden with whatever took our fancy and no doubt looked over by the dearly departed, we all indulged in a sumptuous array of confectionary spiced with laughter and conversation.

With the radio exposure, more and more people wanted to hear what Tabaash had to say, so we hired a theatre in the Buckle Street Museum that was at the time our national museum in Wellington. It was an art deco in design and could sit comfortably 200 people. That was the start of what began as Tabaash's "Medi Teachings" a combination of teaching and meditation. We ran these meetings over a period of twelve years. To begin with, we did these fortnightly which I changed to monthly as it was all getting a bit too much with everything else. We booked the theatre for the whole year and had pocket sized calendars printed so it was easy for people to pop them into their handbag or wallet. I liked to use about ten minutes of the meeting at the start to promote others people's work and came up with the idea to have a "light worker" talk to the audience about themselves and the work they were doing.

This proved popular as it was a good platform to get some exposure. I recall one evening when we arrived, and the security guard would not let any of us in as he said our name was not down on the list. I showed him the calendar proving that we had booked the whole year, but he was not having a bar of it. The guy was only doing his job, but I was really pissed off, and there were 200 people all hanging around. So what did we do? Well, it was a nice warm summer's evening, and there were some nice long steps at the front of the museum, so that seemed the obvious choice! So Tabaash stood on the road that ran in front of the museum. It wasn't a public road but one that simply took you to the car park. There was no traffic at that time of the night but the milkman and his cart kept driving through, and every time he did Tabaash would give him a hearty greeting and bow to him!

The museum closed down to be turned into a university, and so we moved to the National Library theatre where we continued the meetings. Tabaash loved using interesting music in his meditations. He would weave a story around the music taking the audience through all sorts of journeys. H would send me on music missions where I would poke around the local CD shops in the search of interesting music to use. One time as I was walking through town he told me that there was a certain CD he wanted to use, and he told me where to get it. I went into the shop and asked where I could find it. The guy looked up on his computer and said that it wasn't listed so it wasn't in the shop. I told him that I knew it was there and had that information on good authority. He looked at me like I was something demented, but he did humour me and have a closer inspection, and funny, he found it!

We started those meetings also in Christchurch in the South Island of New Zealand and found a great modern theatre and a fantastic bed and breakfast across the road where we could stay. We had started offering personal one-on-one sessions with Tabaash before we had started the big meetings, and so the profile was building. I think back now on those years of those public meetings and remember with gratitude and love the many people whom we met and who supported our journey. At the end of the day it's all about the people and all about the union we all create by our common interest in developing in the way we are. I feel very humbled by all of this.

I've been a very fortunate man to be able to have a job that I really love that allows me to meet every day the most extraordinary people and to do something that is assisting in the raising of consciousness. And more than that, I have been able to experience first-hand that "something more" that I always knew existed.

And it is real, and it is wonderful, and I can tell you right here and know that we have nothing to fear when we die. When I channel, I go to that "house" that I first met Tabaash in. There are always teachers and guides who are there for me, and sometimes I will meet up with large groups of souls, and we will go to places on Earth where there is conflict, and we will transmit energy to heal that conflict. It's a busy place out there in spirit, believe you me.

There have been times when I have been assigned a personal mission, for a specific person. I realize now that we are all guides for each other, regardless of the fact that we are in bodies or out of bodies, and so one day when I was "out there," I was told that I had to go and assist a young man who was considering suicide. He lived in New York, and I went to his apartment and from my vantage point (it felt like I was looking down on him from the corner of the ceiling), I could see him sitting in a chair, and he had a gun in his hand. He was in his early twenties, and I could feel his despair. It was like a wave of energy that was emitting from his whole being.

I concentrated hard on him, sending him waves of peace and love, forming in my thoughts the idea that there were better ways for him and that he did not have to take such a drastic step. I formed this and sent this to him with all the love I could muster.

He picked up on this as he suddenly sat up and said, "Who's there?"

So he must have sensed that I was there though he would not have known it was I, of course. He sat back down again, but this time he put the gun on the table beside the chair. He stood up and started to pace around the room, still feeling agitated, but I could see that he was calming down. I kept my vigil; time was irrelevant. After a while he started to ask God for help. This is always a good sign as the moment you do that, you have opened up the channels of life that will help you. As he put the thought out to God, I was able to send source energy to him that calmed him even more, and he was able to start thinking in a more logical way. The extreme emotions that he had been feeling started to dissipate. He went to the window and he looked out. He saw a friend of his walk by, and the friend looked up and waved for him to come down. He turned and looked at the gun on the table, went over to it, and then locked it away. He walked out of his apartment and went to join his friend, and my job was done.

That experience made me think differently about the way we are guided and helped. I realized that since we were all spirit, living out all realities we had created, then we really were always helping each other. There will never be any point in our lives where we don't have access to all forms of guidance. Isn't that comforting knowing that we are being cared for and loved all the time? Of course, people's issues can take them to such emotional extremes where they shut out all assistance and, therefore, suffer the consequences. Regardless of that fact, there is always hope, always guidance and always love available in the worst-case scenarios that some may create.

I find it hard it hard to believe that I have been the channel for Tabaash for over twenty years now. It struck me the other day how long I had been doing this when a young woman in her late teens came and had a session with Tabaash, and I recalled that Tabaash had done a blessing at her christening! Tabaash has done naming ceremonies and weddings over the years. We have done many seminars on a variety of subjects. My work has taken me offshore, and I have had the great privilege of working with other people who are also involved helping to raise awareness.

Doing these things at times puts you into rather bizarre and funny situations. A woman approached me and said that she was changing her name and that she wanted Tabaash to do a naming ceremony for her. This was all very well and then she said that she wanted to be completely immersed in water. I looked out the window. It was the height of winter, a cold wind southerly was blowing, and the sea was hardly going to be tropical temperatures. Nevertheless, I agreed but insisted we do it where we were all warm! In the end she hired a unit in a hotel which had a hot pool. I was trying so hard not to laugh as fully clad I stood up to my waist in warm bubbling water before bringing Tabaash through. He took it all in his stride, spoke the most beautiful of words, and then while she held her nose he plunged her under the water and brought her up again.

Another situation was at a wedding. Tabaash had written the ceremony for the couple and duly performed it. However, the couple decided that they would not inform guests and family that Tabaash was, in fact, a spirit channelled through me. This was mainly due to the fact that some of the relatives would not have approved. Afterwards when I had returned, people were coming up to me and asking me where I was from as my accent was so different. When Tabaash uses my body there are always a few subtle changes, the voice being one of those. Some have referred to it as Tabaash's accent, but it's actually an inflection brought about by the way spirit is manipulating my vocal chords. Since I as Blair am not there to speak as I would, Tabaash simply organizes the voice. I also get quite shiny when I am channelling, particularly when I do public work. When I asked Tabaash about that, he told me that God's light shines through me. When we do public work, the energy is more intensified, and, therefore, the light shines brighter.

I always feel really energized after my day's work of channelling, and even when I have channelled for a long time during a seminar, I still feel the same way. I feel the need to get grounded though, hence my gym workouts or my power-walks up bush to be amongst nature. There have been times when having channelled for the day I have had to get in the car and drive somewhere, and as I am driving along the motorway, it suddenly strikes me as totally ridiculous and funny that half an hour ago I was out there in spirit just being a soul and now here I was in a car, foot on the accelerator doing a very human thing! Actually I have to be careful driving, particularly on long trips, especially if I am on my own; it's very easy for me to trance-out as driving the car can have a slight hypnotic effect on me. I have let Tabaash drive once or twice, and he is probably more vigilant then I am!

As a human being I have always felt more comfortable simply doing what I do and getting on with the job. I like to drive my own ship and have never wanted to be surrounded by lots of people or be a part of big corporations, etc. I like it uncomplicated and orderly, peaceful and harmonious. Stepping out and doing more has always been a big challenge, and perhaps that attitude has been a hindrance to me as well. Many people have asked why I haven't put out CDs or written books and done the merchandising thing. It never felt comfortable doing those things. It's nice to make a living by doing something that you enjoy, but I never felt at ease with exorbitant prices and pens with Tabaash written on them.

I like to make myself available to all people, as I truly believe it was a good thing to do. The unfortunate thing about that is that you can draw in people who take complete advantage of that and expect everything all the time.

For twelve years I put aside the time between 8-8:30 a.m. for people who have had sessions with Tabaash to ring if there were any questions they needed to ask. There was no fee for this, and I was happy to do this. Then I started getting calls from people who had never even been to see us, and they said their friends told them that they could ring up and have a free session with Tabaash. On being told that wasn't the case and explaining to them about the morning calls, some were quite abusive and downright rude. One woman ranted on about how I wasn't very spiritual and if I was there to help people, then why was I refusing. I hung up on her in mid rant. In the years of channelling Tabaash I have been stalked and abused, raved at and accused of profiteering from people's pain and misery.

Eventually I stopped doing those morning calls as the same people were ringing up with the same issues, and the ones that really should have been ringing never did because they did not want to bother me. Well, I wish some of them had. Some, no doubt, believe that it's not Tabaash at all but me as Blair simply making this all up and acting out some sort of role. It's been quite an exhausting process at times dealing with people's response to who you are and what you do. I recall going to a gallery where a good friend was having an exhibition opening. I was minding my own business with glass of wine in hand, and this woman came up to me and we started chatting. After a while she asked me what I did, and I told her that I was a channel for spirit.

She said aloud, "You're the channel for Tabaash, aren't you?"

Then she just started crying! A friend of hers saw this and came over to comfort her and looked at me with daggers saying, "What did you say to her to make her upset?"

The woman who was crying said to her friend that it was ok I hadn't upset her. It was just that she was overwhelmed by the energy of spirit when she realized who I was. By the look the friend gave me, I could tell she wasn't buying that one!

It was like the school playground all over again, being ignored and standing alone with all your differences. I didn't really mind in the least, but it does make you wary about telling people what you do at times for fear of the reaction. I know of one well-known psychic here in New Zealand who has been physically assaulted by someone who didn't agree with who she was and what she did. Some people make me feel very sad at times.

People's fears and ignorance can make me feel very, very tired at times, and I have to admit I have often wondered if what we are offering is useful to people. I can see in some right away that they are so involved in their need to be victims that despite the efforts they make in changing, that will never happen.

I've asked Tabaash about this and he said, "Do your job and what people do with what they gather is entirely their responsibility."

I think that any person who is involved in the well-being of others feels a high level of responsibility to make it all right for those people, and by doing so, that person often ends up playing roles that are beyond the call of duty. I've certainly have had to learn how to create boundaries over the years; if you don't, you get inundated with the most banal issues of human nature, believe me!

There seems to me that there is desperation from some people, and they believe that the answer is going to come from some outside source rather than themselves. As has been said by many in different ways *"It is ourselves that are the revelation."* Looking at that statement makes me remember that anyone who is of service to people in self-development really is there to assist that person in *seeing themselves* in such a way as to enhance their vision of themselves. I cannot and will not for a moment believe that anybody or any system has the answer, and

I am always rather wary of those who profess to have it. Investigate to your utmost, and along the way you always find what resonates and what does not.

Being a spiritual channel for God is obviously the choice that I have made for this lifetime. I can look back now and see the many signals that were pointing me in that direction. First and foremost, it is my service to God, and because I am of the belief that all is God, then I know that I am being of service to everything and everyone. I am defining myself through the experiences that I am having as a channel for spirit, and through those definitions I am able to see what I am all about and what I can be all about. Writing that makes me think of the way that people respond to spiritual things.

I think of over the years how some clients secretly come to see Tabaash and secretly do other spiritual things because they are *afraid* of the reaction from partners and family, etc. Why should anyone have to sneak around as if they are doing something bad? Why should you be deemed extreme or crazy simply because you believe that we have lived in other lifetimes and talk to nature? Why should someone else's ignorance and fear have such influence on so many? There seems to be so many rules that have been created around God to keep humanity in conflict for another millennium or two—rules, of course, created by other human beings. God did not create rules. God created life with love, and if you love and respect that all are doing the same, then you have no need for rules. Structures born from love allows creation of life; structures born from dissention make life confusing and uncertain.

A couple had been coming to see Tabaash for some years, separately. Neither of them wanted the other to know that they were coming to see Tabaash, and, of course, it was not my place to say anything, so I played along while all the time wondering how long spirit would allow this to happen. There was the odd occasion when they had actually booked on the same day but the appointments were either end of the day, so there was no chance of meeting up. Then one day the inevitable happened when they had booked on the same day, and the appointments were one after the other. I usually have half an hour in between clients, so I didn't think that they had a chance of being *"discovered."*

I had finished with the man, and we were walking down the stairs when who should we meet coming up the stairs but his woman who mistook the time and had arrived half an hour early. I was standing behind the man and thought, "Well, this is going to be interesting!"

They stopped and froze and stared at each other.

"What are you doing here?" she asked

"I've been to see Tabaash" came the reply. "But why are you here?" he then asked.

"Well, I've come to see Tabaash as well," said she.

They both burst out laughing as it dawned on them—much to my relief. They still come to see Tabaash as individuals but have also enjoyed some sessions together as well.

Another story is of two brothers who had a massive falling out that separated them and brought a lot of pain to each other and the families involved. They were each consulting Tabaash in their lives, and he had mentioned on numerous occasions the importance of forgiveness and the need to show love and union as brothers once again, but to no avail. Then he said to each of them separately that a situation would be created where they would have to face each other and deal with what had happened. If they could make peace with each other, much would evolve; if not, then they would never see each other again, and they would have to resolve the issue in another lifetime. What happened was that they were both making an offshore trip and unbeknownst to either of them, they were going to the same place and were booked on the same flight. Tabaash had *"organized"* for them to be sitting next to each other. One of the brothers was already settled and no doubt wondering who would be his flight companion. He looked up to see his brother coming down the aisle, stop at where he was to sit, look up to make sure the number was correct, and then burst out laughing.

At the same time they looked at each other and said, "Bloody Tabaash!"

I really loved that story, and the end result was exceptionally positive I am glad to say.

Listening to the advice and living the advice in our everyday life and occurrences is what being God is all about. You cannot say you are God and still carry hate for someone. That is not being God. That is being human in your nature. You cannot go to all the development courses, pick up new tools, love people, say you are God and then go and self-harm or shoot people or smack your wife around. That is not being God. Practicing being God in everyday life is actually easier than creating big things you feel you need to do or become or experience.

I've been fortunate to collaborate with some amazingly gifted light workers whose diverse talents have given so much life to people. One of these people is a dear friend of mine, Hetty Rodenburg, who is a doctor, and she has taken the powerful step of being very open about her own spiritual journey and has incorporated this in her work. She was a close friend of Elizabeth Kubler-Ross who was the pioneer for modern day hospice care and has facilitated Kubler-Ross workshops worldwide. Hetty and Tabaash have presented a seminar in New Zealand called Travelling Light that is on Grief and Spirituality. Hetty and Tabaash have a wonderful rapport, and they spark off each other magically! I have at times felt sorry for her as I know she has set material she likes to cover in the seminar, whereas Tabaash pretty well decides at the time what he wants to say and will through the day chop and change and swerve here and there leaving poor, no doubt exasperated Hetty having to change her tactics!

I have often been sitting in the dressing room back stage of a theatre having no idea of what Tabaash is going to talk about and pacing back and forth with nervous energy. I'm about to go on stage and talk to 200 people and have no notes, have done no preparation and hope to hell that it's all going to work. The moment I go on stage and face the audience, I can feel this energy coming into me, and I just know that everything is going to be all right. When I first started to do meetings, I always made sure the lights were down so I couldn't see anybody, as I found that if I could, it would distract me, and I would always notice someone who was looking up at the ceiling or chewing their finger! They were probably just listening, but it's those sorts of things that you notice! Not that it put me off, but it was rather disconcerting. As I gained more confidence, I made myself keep the lights on and made a conscious effort of learning to speak to the audience face to face. Before I brought Tabaash through, I would spend five or ten minutes with them—telling some story about my week or some funny little incident or observation. It made me feel more of a part of it, and many people said afterwards how much they enjoyed spending time with me before Tabaash came through. It's an odd sort of job just stepping aside and letting someone else do all the work!

You do have a few people who don't respect boundaries, of course, and can't or won't discern that Tabaash is Tabaash and Blair is Blair. It's not unusual in group social gatherings that someone will come up to me and start asking for personal advice. Once when I was away doing a weekend seminar, I was having a nice quiet dinner on my own, having had a very busy day. One of the seminar participants made a beeline for me and asked if he could join me, and before I could say anything, he had already made himself quite comfortable and for the next two hours pretty well gave me a dissertation on his unhappy love life. He didn't really seem to want an answer; he just talked pretty well non-stop. I made all the right noises and listened. After he finished, he suddenly stopped, stood up and said how much better he felt and what a great job I was doing and then he walked away. I sort of froze in mid-sip of my wine and stared as he walked away and then laughed. I didn't even know his name.

When I was doing the morning calls, someone rang up in such great distress they were sobbing into the phone. I had no idea who it was or even if it was male or female. Then I just got all this information to relay to them and just did so over the next five minutes. The person calmed down after a while, and I finished relaying the information and then asked if it was helpful.

Whoever it was said, "Thank you so much. I really feel better. You have helped me a lot," and then they hung up.

Kay asked me, "Who was that?"

I replied, "Well, I really have no idea, but it seemed to help"!

I have found myself time and time again placed in situations where someone has needed some sort of guidance. On a plane on the way to visit my parents in Auckland, I sat next to someone whose son was going through a great deal, and I was able to pass on information that would assist. At the gym on a bike doing cardio next to some guy who asked me what I did as job and when I told him, he was really interested and asked me how it worked. The moment he did that, all this information that was very relevant to something in his life poured out of me. He sort of went really pale, then burst into tears. We went and talked for about an hour, and it gave him the answers he needed. I suppose when you are here to serve, God is going to keep directing you to those who need it! And what this has shown me is how easy it really is to be your brother's keeper in everyday life. A word here, a reminder there, encouragements and hugs, all of those things are good daily fodder for us all through the day, and it seems easy to get these things when we allow ourselves to be open.

Ok, I have had people cross the street because they have been afraid that I am suddenly going to "read them." Several times when people have come to see Tabaash, they have told me as Blair that they wanted to come ages ago, but they were afraid of what Tabaash was going to say to them.

And I said, "Well, he would only talk to you about your life."

And often the reply was "That's what I am afraid of!"

And then you have those who wanted to come again having had a session maybe three months previously but they were afraid to because they had not followed the advice Tabaash had given them, and they thought they were going to be told off! Spirit does not ever tell anyone off. They only encourage you to persevere and support you in your endeavours. And they do it with great love and respect for the choices that you are making in your life.

As Tabaash likes to say, "Well, you were just God doing it that way."

God, I would be in constant detention if that were the case having not followed at times advice spirit has given me! We are not here to be punished by higher sources; we are here to be loved, guided and honoured by them. Our own ideas of ourselves do the entire punishing that is needed, and we have to stop that, as it is so exhausting.

Conceive of the idea that we are all and everything, and that there is no need to encourage indemnity against self-punishment. Self-punishment only occurs when you believe you have wronged, and you can never be wrong as you are God, and a God would only love.

TABAASH SPEAKS

You can only be what you decide, and it is the decisions that you have made from the very time that you ever became that have established all your journeys wherever they have taken you through your history. Human beings on Earth are being faced with some big choices now, and it starts off with each of you making the decision about yourself. Making the decisions about yourself will determine the future of this planet and the way life will be, and all of you now are carrying the thread of this. As you each make your choices, you weave the future of Earth and what its story is to be. It is not a big responsibility that you all carry but simply this part of the story that you have come to, and as I have mentioned before, there will always be many futures. You cannot be without God, be you on Earth or beyond: it is simply impossible to conceive of harmony without living the energy of God. That is true enough when one looks upon the suffering that has occurred throughout the history on Earth. You cannot dilute God with human ideas that bring about discrepancies that separate people into unfair factions.

You are not doing a thing wrong. You are living out what you have created and what you have decided, and now it is time to look upon how what was can no longer be the same, and so you are simply faced with making a decision. Live daily as God in the way that you know you can, and by doing so, you are doing enough. If you wish to do more than enough, then make sure that what you do is never overwhelming you. It should always be a pleasant journey where along the way you have a great deal of fun.

We love you, and we are your constant companions through life.

Tabaash

CHAPTER TWELVE

What's around the corner?

Unknown

I am always aware that my choice to be a channel for spirit will present me to myself in a very amplified way. I am God yes, doing the work that I do in life, but I am also a man who is living his life and being aware of his faults and wanting to improve his ideas, his ways, his life. Being of service to God does not make you infallible. I make mistakes and get pissed off and swear at people who do stupid things on the road. I cry, I hurt, I bleed and I am afraid at times. I'm hard on myself and think too much about stuff that I shouldn't need to think about. I get impatient and stressed and wonder what the hell is going on. I am accountable and I know that. Letting yourself down when you know better is the worst of things as others who have done so, can attest to. And yet when we do see and we do know what steps to take, then we can see how much we can make it all better.

Being a spiritual being does not mean we *STOP* being a human being; it just means that we have the power to stop ourselves from making choices that will not serve us and ultimately anyone else, and as we have seen through history, we have to do it a few times before we get it. When the intention is there to change, we have to strike a deal with our ultimate selves and create the ultimate ideas that match. Then, of course, we have to daily practice those ideas and at times in the face of adversity.

Three years ago my wife was diagnosed with Alzheimer's, and it has thrown me into the present. It is the only genuine place to be when you are dealing with such a thing. It has made me sit up and pay more attention to who I am and what I am doing; it has made me listen more and be a better man. It has also created sadness, anxiety and worry. It has made me at times feel helpless and blank, knowing that the inevitable conclusion is that she is going away from me. When she is having a bad day, I look in her beautiful face and see her fear and her confusion; it is like looking at an animal that is trapped in a cage. It is also a tender and loving experience full of laughter and honesty that brings out the authenticity in each other. I have become her dresser, her cook and cleaner, her makeup artist and hairdresser, I am her domestic God. Being everything for one person makes you more conscious of having all of your selves on call all the time, and you're never quite sure which one or ones will be called upon to give service.

So what's out there? Why everything, of course! What shall I do with it? Why whatever I choose.

And that is another future in my story.

THE LAST WORD

There will always be people who disagree with who you are and what you think and what you will do.

At times you will be challenged with this in your life, but turning the other cheek is not the answer.

There are non-aggressive ways that allow you to stand up to your adversaries so that the energy bullies do not overwhelm you.

They are not wrong. They are simply being, feeling and expressing what they believe to be right.

Right is only right because that is what they have invested in.

If you invest in believing that what you are is profound and powerful ambitious and successful,

You will succeed with all your ideas, and you make being the ultimate creator your natural ambition.

Turning the other cheek only shows you the view from that angle.

Stand up to life and don't put up with a thing, for putting up only puts you down.

Standing up in life makes you taller and shows you all the view.

When you do that, you are not small. You are all.

About the Author

Blair Styra was born in Canada in 1960 and spent the first eleven years of his life there. In 1971 he and his family immigrated to Auckland New Zealand. Always feeling he had a close connection with God he eventually discovered his ability as a spiritual channel for a spirit energy known as Tabaash in the 1980s. In the 1990s he went public with Tabaash and has been working as a full time channel since then. His work has taken him throughout New Zealand and offshore. Blair presently lives in Wellington New Zealand.

www.tabaash.com

Other Books By Ozark Mountain Publishing, Inc.

Dolores Cannon
Conversations with Nostradamus,
  Volume I, II, III
Jesus and the Essenes
They Walked with Jesus
Between Death and Life
A Soul Remembers Hiroshima
Keepers of the Garden.
The Legend of Starcrash
The Custodians
The Convoluted Universe - Book One,
  Two, Three, Four
Five Lives Remembered
The Three Waves of Volunteers and the
  New Earth
Stuart Wilson & Joanna Prentis
The Essenes - Children of the Light
Power of the Magdalene
Beyond Limitations
Atlantis and the New Consciousness
The Magdalene Version
O.T. Bonnett, M.D./Greg Satre
Reincarnation: The View from Eternity
What I Learned After Medical School
Why Healing Happens
M. Don Schorn
Elder Gods of Antiquity
Legacy of the Elder Gods
Gardens of the Elder Gods
Reincarnation...Stepping Stones of Life
Aron Abrahamsen
Holiday in Heaven
Out of the Archives – Earth Changes
Sherri Cortland
Windows of Opportunity
Raising Our Vibrations for the New Age
The Spiritual Toolbox
Michael Dennis
Morning Coffee with God
God's Many Mansions
Nikki Pattillo
Children of the Stars
A Spiritual Evolution
Rev. Grant H. Pealer
Worlds Beyond Death
A Funny Thing Happened on the Way to
  Heaven
Maiya & Geoff Gray-Cobb
Angels - The Guardians of Your Destiny
Maiya Gray-Cobb
Seeds of the Soul
Sture Lönnerstrand
I Have Lived Before
Arun & Sunanda Gandhi
The Forgotten Woman
Claire Doyle Beland
Luck Doesn't Happen by Chance

James H. Kent
Past Life Memories As A Confederate
  Soldier
Dorothy Leon
Is Jehovah An E.T
Justine Alessi & M. E. McMillan
Rebirth of the Oracle
Donald L. Hicks
The Divinity Factor
Christine Ramos, RN
A Journey Into Being
Mary Letorney
Discover The Universe Within You
Debra Rayburn
Let's Get Natural With Herbs
Jodi Felice
The Enchanted Garden
Susan Mack & Natalia Krawetz
My Teachers Wear Fur Coats
Ronald Chapman
Seeing True
Rev. Keith Bender
The Despiritualized Church
Vara Humphreys
The Science of Knowledge
Karen Peebles
The Other Side of Suicide
Antoinette Lee Howard
Journey Through Fear
Julia Hanson
Awakening To Your Creation
Irene Lucas
Thirty Miracles in Thirty Days
Mandeep Khera
Why?
Robert Winterhalter
The Healing Christ
James Wawro
Ask Your Inner Voice
Tom Arbino
You Were Destined to be Together
Maureen McGill & Nola Davis
Live From the Other Side
Anita Holmes
TWIDDERS
Walter Pullen
Evolution of the Spirit
Cinnamon Crow
Teen Oracle
Chakra Zodiac Healing Oracle
Jack Churchward
Lifting the Veil on the Lost Continent of
  Mu

For more information about any of the above titles, soon to be released titles,
or other items in our catalog, write or visit our website:
PO Box 754, Huntsville, AR 72740
www.ozarkmt.com

Other Books By Ozark Mountain Publishing, Inc.

Guy Needler
The History of God
Beyond the Source – Book 1,2
Dee Wallace/Jarred Hewett
The Big E
Dee Wallace
Conscious Creation
Natalie Sudman
Application of Impossible Things
Henry Michaelson
And Jesus Said – A Conversation
Victoria Pendragon
SleepMagic
Riet Okken
The Liberating Power of Emotions
Janie Wells
Payment for Passage
Dennis Wheatley/ Maria Wheatley
The Essential Dowsing Guide
Dennis Milner
Kosmos
Garnet Schulhauser
Dancing on a Stamp
Julia Cannon
Soul Speak – The Language of Your
     Body
Charmian Redwood
Coming Home to Lemuria
Kathryn Andries
Soul Choices – 6 Paths to Find Your Life
     Purpose

For more information about any of the above titles, soon to be released titles,
or other items in our catalog, write or visit our website:
PO Box 754, Huntsville, AR 72740
www.ozarkmt.com